Letters to My Son: Volume 1

Looking for a Godly Life Partner

Nii Lante Wallace-Bruce, PhD

KINGDOM BOOKS

Copyright © Nii Lante Wallace-Bruce, 2017

Published by Kingdom Books, an imprint of *CreativeJuicesBooks, Singapore (www.creativejuicesbooks.com)*

All rights reserved. Except for brief quotations in printed reviews, no part of this book may be reproduced, stored in a retrieval system, or transmitted in any form or by any means—electronic, mechanical, digital, photocopy, recording, or any other—without prior permission in writing from the publisher.

All Scripture quotations, unless otherwise indicated, are taken from the *New King James Version*®. Copyright © 1982 by Thomas Nelson. Used by permission. All rights reserved.

Scripture quotations marked *NLT* are taken from the *Holy Bible, New Living Translation*, copyright © 1996, 2004, 2007 by Tyndale House Foundation. Used by permission of Tyndale House Publishers, Inc., Carol Stream, Illinois 60188. All rights reserved.

Scripture quotations marked *NIV* are taken from the *Holy Bible: New International Version* ®. Copyright © 1973, 1978, 1984 International Bible Society. Used by permission of Zondervan Bible Publishers. All rights reserved.

Scriptures marked *GW* are taken from *God's Word*®, © 1995 *God's Word to the Nations*. Used by permission of Baker Publishing Group.

National Library Board, Singapore Cataloguing-in-Publication Data

Name(s): Wallace-Bruce, Nii Lante
Title: Looking for a Godly Life Partner / Nii Lante Wallace-Bruce.
Description: Singapore: published by Kingdom Books, an
　　imprint of CreativeJuicesBooks, [2017]
Identifier(s): OCN 974004945 | ISBN 978-981-11-2892-9 (paperback)
Subject(s): LCSH: Mate selection--Religious aspects--Christianity.
　　| Man-woman relationships--Religious aspects--Christianity.
　　| Marriage--Religious aspects--Christianity.
Classification: DDC 248.844--dc23

Contents

Acknowledgments v

Introduction to the Series vii

PART A: LAYING YOUR OWN FOUNDATIONS

1 A Solid Foundation in Life Is Absolutely Essential 3

2 Above All, Lay a Solid Spiritual Foundation 10

3 Know Yourself Very Well 15

PART B: COMMENCING THE SEARCH

4 Do You Really Have to Start a Relationship Now? 27

5 How to Go about Choosing a Life Partner Today 34

6 Don't Go on a Wild Goose Chase 40

7 Qualities to Look for and How to Go about It 45

PART C: GETTING TO KNOW YOUR PARTNER

8 Commencing an Exploratory Friendship 61

9 Turning the Friendship into a Relationship 69

PART D: MAKING IT THROUGH THE COURTSHIP

10 Learn Early to Give and Take   *87*

11 Learn the Balancing Act   *96*

12 Seek Crucial Clearances   *103*

PART E: PREPARING FOR MARRIAGE

13 Start Marriage Preparations   *121*

14 Follow Family Protocol   *126*

15 Finish with God's Blessings   *130*

16 Don't Allow Yourself to Get Desperate   *133*

About the Author   *140*

Your Next Step   *141*

Acknowledgments

*I would like to express my sincere appreciation to Ms Ursula Lang and her editorial team for putting it all together so beautifully—God bless you all.
My gratitude also goes to all others who contributed to bringing this book to print.*

Indeed, I am also grateful for the support of my family, particularly my life partner Victoria and my son Nii.

Introduction to the Series

Today, there are those who say that marriage is out of fashion... They say that it is not worth making a life-long commitment, making a definitive decision, "for ever", because we do not know what tomorrow will bring. I ask you, instead, to be revolutionaries, I ask you to swim against the tide; yes, I am asking you to rebel against this culture that sees everything as temporary and that ultimately believes you are incapable of responsibility, that believes you are incapable of true love.

Pope Francis

Life is all about relationships, and being in the right set of relationships can help one to progress in life and achieve destiny and greatness. On the other hand, being in wrong relationships can slow a person down and put a limitation on one's progress and achievement of destiny—or even wreck it altogether. Finding a life partner and getting married are two of the most critical steps one will ever take as regards relationships in particular and life in general; they are destiny-defining steps.

This book is the first in a series which offers practical guidance to readers on entering into and enjoying life-long marriage relationships. The books are written from a Christian perspective, but they can be helpful to all who desire to build happy marriages that last a lifetime.

The title of this series, *Letters to My Son*, may sound strange. I am writing these books for two main reasons. First, my background qualifies me to write on such a topic. I am an experienced lawyer, author and international evangelist, teaching and preaching in various countries. I have a particular passion for the subject matter of these books.

The second reason for writing these books is that I have a son who is in his twenties. He lives in Australia and he is settled; he has a good job and has bought himself an apartment in the inner city of Brisbane, Australia. It is a nice apartment with glimpses of the Brisbane River.

My son has mentioned to me that he wants to get married, apparently because a number of his friends have got married or are planning to do so in the near future. We have talked about it and it has made me to think more deeply about the subject. This has prompted me to carry out further research into the subject of marriage, resulting in my writing this series of books.

I used to work with the United Nations in peacekeeping. As I was based in Sudan and my son was thousands of miles away in Australia, I believed that the most effective way to convey my messages on relationships to him was by way of letters akin to the letters which the Apostle Paul wrote to the early churches. The objective was to provide him with detailed practical guidance on entering into and enjoying a lifelong marriage relationship.

Introduction to the Series

Although it was my son's quest for advice and guidance that led me to write these books, I have not limited them to his personal circumstances only. Rather, I have written the books in such a way as to appeal to all single men and women who are looking for life partners and who would like to proceed to marriage and would like to remain married.

To put it another way, the books are written to provide practical guidance to any person who is starting on the journey of a lifetime of relationship, beginning with finding a life partner, progressing to marriage, and then remaining in that marriage and enjoying it thoroughly.

PART A

LAYING YOUR OWN FOUNDATIONS

Chapter 1

A Solid Foundation in Life Is Absolutely Essential

The foundation stones for a balanced success are honesty, character, integrity, faith, love and loyalty.

Zig Ziglar

I will come to the subject matter of looking for the right life partner later, but let us first consider some fundamentals of life.

Laying a solid foundation generally

To succeed at anything in life, you must first lay a solid foundation. Take the process of building a house, for example; you must first lay a solid foundation, so that the structure you put up can withstand not only rough weather but also the test of time generally. A sober person does not start building a house and say, "Today I do not have much money but I need a house to sleep in, so I will just build something useful and not worry too much about the foundation, as I will improve on it as time goes by."

No, it does not work that way. The risk you take is too much, as your house could be blown away within days, weeks or months by rough weather. To build a good and proper house, you should not cut corners.

If you are not ready to lay a solid foundation, then it is better that you wait and take your time to ensure that, when you are ready to start, you will be able to build a strong foundation. Sometimes, you may have to construct that foundation bit by bit; but, nevertheless, when you are done with it, you have to ensure that it is solid.

I also need not remind you that, if you are planning to build a structure of more than one level, the foundation has to be even deeper and stronger; otherwise, a small tilt at the top can seriously affect the whole edifice. You can imagine how deep and solid the foundations of some tall buildings are—especially those skyscrapers in New York, Dubai, Shanghai, Hong Kong and other cities in the world.

Bear in mind also that, in certain parts of the world, heavy rainfalls, floods and even cyclones are common; so a solid foundation is needed all the more. Houses on solid foundations may get battered by storms, but they will still remain standing; whereas those on weak foundations will collapse, or get blown away, and you see them floating in the flood waters.

Here in Darfur where I work, the same thing happens. When a *haboob* (heavy sandstorm) strikes, some houses are decapitated (with the roofs being blown miles away), others are reduced to shadows of themselves, and yet others disappear with little or no trace.

The point I am making is that, when you are building a house, it is absolutely essential to lay a solid foundation, so that the house can stand the test of time. The same goes for any other human endeavour.

Laying a solid foundation cannot be compromised; it is absolutely essential in every area of life. If you desire to be good in your career (be it in banking, law, engineering, ministry or some other profession), you need a solid foundation. This should start with obtaining a good education in your chosen field and getting good coaching, experience and mentorship. This is an initial but critical investment. Once you have that, you can build on it, and you can then expect to begin climbing the career ladder.

In short, everything in life requires you to start with a solid foundation, and then you build on it as you go along.

The solid foundation should be broad-based

Coming back to the analogy of building a house, the foundation which is laid has to be broad-based, to ensure that the weight of the building is distributed over a wide area and not confined to only certain parts. The builder has to ensure that the building will have stability and resistance. Therefore, the load should be spread over the whole surface area to ensure that, as the building starts to go up, every part of it will rest on a solid foundation.

It is the same with life generally. You have to lay a solid foundation, not only in certain areas of your life but all of it. The foundation you lay has to cover every aspect of your life; it has to be total and solid in every part. The approach has to be holistic. This is because, if one aspect is weak, it can set back the other parts or even bring the whole structure down.

For example, people who lay a solid foundation for a career (obtaining excellent education, training and so on) but have not done the same for other areas of their lives will with time—while making progress in their careers—find themselves facing setbacks in those other areas. The end result is that, overall, they are not making as much progress in life as they would desire, because there are weaknesses in some aspects of their lives.

Then you will hear such people complaining that they have invested so much into their education, gone to the best schools, and yet life is still not going well for them. The reason probably is that the foundation they have laid is lopsided—solid in one area but weak or virtually non-existent in others. So, in order to avoid this, one should lay a foundation which is not only solid but also broad-based.

In management, there is a concept known as Total Quality Management (TQM). It applies here. One should adopt a holistic approach and lay a foundation in all areas of one's life. The areas I am referring to are:

- ✓ Material
- ✓ Physical
- ✓ Emotional
- ✓ Psychological
- ✓ Social

When you talk about laying a solid foundation in life, a lot of people immediately think of having a good education, a well-paid, high-status job, a nice car, and a nice place to sleep (if you are buying a house, it is even better). To them, you will then be on your way up. All these are indeed fine and to be commended, but they cover only one area of life; I put them under what I refer to as the "**Material Aspect**".

The **Physical Aspect** is equally important. You should start laying a foundation of good physical health at an early age and build on it as life progresses. Unfortunately, some people take this aspect of life for granted; they have no strategy or plan for it. They just go through life, hoping that everything will be fine. It is only when something goes awry with their health that they realize they have neglected the physical aspect of their lives. That is when they begin to seek information on gyms, exercises, physical fitness coaches and the rest.

What I am saying is that the physical aspect of life is very important and a solid foundation should be laid in this area, starting at an early age. It should become part and parcel of one's lifestyle; this requires consistency.

Maintain a regular keep-fit regime: walk, jog or swim; play games like soccer, rugby and cricket; work out at the gym. These are all good for laying and maintaining a solid foundation for the physical aspect of life. So keep it up!

Laying a solid foundation in this area also includes living a healthy lifestyle. Avoid the couch potato syndrome (spending too much time in front of the TV) and over-dependence on fast foods. It is important to have a nutritious and balanced diet too.

Next are the **Emotional and Psychological Aspects**. We need to be emotionally and psychologically stable. The storms of life will come from time to time, and we should be able to withstand them. We should be mentally alert and strong. We cannot go about life with confidence if we are not psychologically and emotionally stable. Any difficulties or problems in these areas can have serious drawbacks on our overall progress in life. By their nature, challenges in these areas may not be easily detected. However, once they come to light, all efforts should be made to address them. Issues with anger, self-discipline, self-esteem and the like should not be allowed to fester but should be nipped in the bud.

Then there is the **Social Aspect**. We lay a solid foundation in this area by acquiring social skills and learning to interact with people, and not by becoming a recluse, social outcast or lone ranger. Sure, some people are born extroverts and others introverts, but you will learn in life that it is very important to be able to mix with people, talk to them, and socialize (with the right people, of course). You will gain the necessary social and people skills to do this by laying a solid foundation early.

****

There is one more aspect which should be included in the laying of a solid foundation. Because of its importance, I have devoted the whole of the next chapter to it.

A Solid Foundation in Life Is Absolutely Essential

Key Points to Remember

1. To make it in life and achieve one's destiny, one has to lay a solid foundation for life.
2. A life without a solid foundation can be vulnerable to the vicissitudes of life.
3. That foundation should be holistic in approach and should cover all important aspects of life.
4. The earlier one does this the better, and then one can build on it as time goes by.

Questions to Ponder

i. What steps have you taken or are taking towards laying a solid foundation for the Material Aspects of your life?
ii. Are you aware of any Emotional or Psychological challenges in your life? If so, what steps have you taken to address them?
iii. Do you have issues with anger, low self-esteem, loneliness or inability to trust people? Do you know the root causes of these issues? What are you doing to address these challenges?
iv. Do you consider yourself to be healthy? What is the basis of your conclusion? If yes, how do you maintain your health? If no, what are you doing about it?
v. Do you mix easily in a group?
vi. Are you able to interact easily with strangers?

CHAPTER 2

Above All, Lay a Solid Spiritual Foundation

For no other foundation can anyone lay than that which is laid, which is Jesus Christ.

1 Corinthians 3:11

Human beings are not just the tangible bodies which we see. They also have souls and spirits which, although invisible, are very important; in fact, powerful. Without the soul and spirit, the body cannot exist. When we say that a person is dead, we mean that the soul and spirit have left the body. It is the body that dies, decomposes and is buried. But the soul and spirit live on; they do not die.

The second point is that a lot of people think we live only in this world, this planet, because that is the tangible one that they can see. However, the truth is that we operate in two realms: the Natural and the Spiritual. All the major religions of the world agree on this.

Our souls and spirits—especially our spirits—are in touch with the spiritual realm. Therefore, it is very important to know how the spiritual realm works and to ensure that you are in touch with it. Unfortunately, many people are oblivious to the spiritual realm, and so they go through life without spiritual direction or meaning.

Three key principles govern the relationship between the spiritual and natural realms:

1. The spirit realm influences and controls what happens in the natural realm;
2. Things happen first in the spiritual realm, and then they simply manifest in the natural;
3. Positive and negative incidents occur in similar ways, with the spiritual happening first, then the natural.

The best illustration of how these principles operate in practice can be found in the Bible, in *2 Kings 6: 8-17*. We are told that the king of Syria, in his exasperation with the prophet Elisha, sent a great army at night against him. The prophet was then in a city called Dothan.

The next morning, when the prophet's servant saw the Syrian army on horses and chariots everywhere, he was very afraid and reported it to his master. However, the prophet calmly told him not to be overly concerned because those defending them were more than the Syrians. But the servant was not convinced, as he could only see in the natural. Looking around him, they seemed to have no defence at all; they appeared to be at the total mercy of the Syrian army.

The prophet prayed to God to open the supernatural eyes of the servant, so that he could see into the spiritual realm. When that happened, lo and behold, the servant could see thousands of horses and chariots of fire ready to defend them. The Syrian army was no match against this vast army.

This story clearly demonstrates that we operate in two realms: one that the natural eye sees; and the other, though not visible to the natural eye, is ever-present and in fact is more important.

Therefore, whenever you get a thought, idea or plan to do anything on this earth, this thought, idea or plan would have entered your spirit from the spiritual realm. That thought simply influences or directs you to do on earth what has already been planned in the spiritual realm or has already taken place there.

Because the spiritual realm influences or determines what we do in the natural world, it goes without saying that, if you are in touch with the spiritual side of life and give it the priority it deserves, you would have a special insight into life. You surely will have a distinct edge over those who have no idea of the spiritual realm and think life is all about the things that they see, feel, hear, smell and touch.

Hence, as a spiritual being (and not just a tangible body), you should lay a solid foundation in the things of the spirit, having a good understanding of how the spiritual realm operates and how it can influence and control the decisions which you think you make in this life.

Good (positive) things that can happen to you will have their origins in the spiritual world. Similarly, bad (negative) things which can happen to you in the natural world will have their origins in the spiritual realm too.

Above All, Lay a Solid Spiritual Foundation

At your age, you would already have had many experiences, some positive, others negative. You would have had some really beautiful seasons, and you would also have had some terrible times. Maybe you have put them down to "good luck" or "bad luck".

But the truth is that they have their origins in the spiritual realm, not what you merely experience in the natural. For example, if you were promised a job or a promotion and then, at the last minute, something went wrong or your employer simply went quiet and you did not hear anything further, the explanation could be spiritual and not merely natural.

Furthermore, you should know that there is a God who created the heavens and the earth. He reigns over His creation and especially the spiritual sphere. Since He is in charge of the spiritual realm, you need to know Him and connect with Him in order to lay a solid spiritual foundation.

To put it another way, you cannot go through life and not have an anchor in spiritual matters—somebody, powerful and reliable, to look after you and your affairs. As part of laying a solid spiritual foundation, you should develop and maintain a firm relationship with God Almighty, so as to ensure that you are not alone in spiritual matters.

KEY POINTS TO REMEMBER

1. Human beings are essentially spiritual beings.

2. A solid foundation for the spiritual aspects of life is thus necessary.

3. Human beings operate in both the natural and spiritual realms, with the latter being more important.

4. A solid foundation in matters spiritual will give you insightful knowledge and understanding of the things which happen around you.

5. You need an anchor in spiritual matters and, since God Almighty is the King of the spiritual realm, you should develop and maintain a close relationship with Him.

QUESTIONS TO PONDER

i. What is your own understanding of the term "spiritual"?

ii. Do you consider yourself spiritual?

iii. What foundations, if any, have you laid in this aspect of your life?

iv. Do you have an intimate relationship with God? Do you commune with Him on a daily basis? How?

Chapter 3

Know Yourself Very Well

Knowing yourself is the beginning of all wisdom.

Aristotle

You have laid the necessary foundations, and things are moving smoothly in life. Now you have reached the point where you feel you should not be alone; you want a life partner. Before we get to discussing how to go about it, let us talk a bit more about yourself.

Before you can think of bringing somebody else into your life, you have to make sure that you know yourself very well: your strengths and weaknesses, hopes and aspirations, and everything else.

Are you ready for marriage? This involves more than having a degree, a good job, some savings, and a house of your own. You should be mentally, physically, spiritually and emotionally prepared to share your life with someone else. This is the time to review the foundations we have spoken about earlier, to make sure that they are all solid. If there is a weakness in any area, it should be addressed now.

For example, do you have issues with anger or self-discipline? Are you able to mix and mingle with people easily, especially people you are meeting for the first time? Are you the kind of person who likes to be on your own most of the time or do you like being with others?

Are you able to plan and manage well or do you need a lot of assistance and encouragement in this area? What about giving to others or helping them? I mean, doing charitable things; does it come to you easily or are you struggling with it?

As you would have learnt by now, life is full of ups and downs, and so you need to make sure you have what it takes to power your way through life no matter what comes at you. If you do not know yourself very well, the enemy will eventually discover your weaknesses and capitalize on them to ensure that you do not progress in life, let alone achieve your destiny.

Know your purpose in life

The central part of knowing yourself is to know your purpose. Do you know your purpose in life? Do you know why you are on this earth? It is essential that you know your purpose as you go through life.

The term "destiny" is often bandied around, but many people do not really understand what it entails. One cannot talk of destiny if one does not know one's purpose in life. It is your purpose that will lead you to achieve your destiny.

I am sure you have heard people asking this perennial question: "What am I on this earth for?" Let me assure you that nobody is here on this earth just for the sake of being here. It is not by mere coincidence that you or I or anyone we know or care about is on this planet at this very point in time.

Every one of us is here for a reason and every one of us has a purpose. The One who created us gave each one of us a purpose in life. It is fulfilling that purpose that will lead us to fulfilling our destiny.

Going through life without knowing your purpose is like trying to live your life without direction; it is like a ship moving about in the ocean without a compass. It would just be going round in circles and be unlikely to reach its destination. Similarly, an airplane which does not have a compass or modern navigation devices will not be able to fly to where it is supposed to go. In fact, it is questionable whether it would be able to take off from the ground in the first place.

You may be asking, "So how do I know my purpose?" Finding your purpose in life is not as complicated as people may think. For some, they were told at the outset. Jeremiah, for example, was called at a very young age to be a prophet:

> Then the word of the LORD came to me, saying:
> "Before I formed you in the womb I knew you; before you were born I sanctified you; I ordained you a prophet to the nations."
> *Jeremiah 1:4-5*

Our purpose in life was determined before we were birthed on earth; this is all part of God's grand design for His creation. For some, like the prophet Jeremiah, their purpose was revealed to them early in life.

Of course, this makes life straightforward for them. Before both John the Baptist and Jesus Christ were birthed on this earth, God had already announced what they would be coming to earth for. Not only that, He proclaimed it hundreds of years ahead through His prophets, especially Isaiah.

Many others discover their purpose with time. It is better to find out later than not at all—and, hopefully, you will not discover your purpose only when your time on this earth is almost over. That would be a total waste of your life.

If you do not yet know your purpose in life, I strongly recommend that you give it absolute priority now. Find out exactly why your Creator put you on this earth. You are definitely not here merely for the sake of being here; or because a spermatozoa from your father was fast enough to strike an egg in your mother's womb.

Science will tell you that that is how it happened. But, you remember our discussion in the previous chapter, on the spiritual aspect of life? It just did not happen that way; it was not by chance or coincidence or the pleasure of your parents. Rather, that arrangement was made first in the spirit before it was manifested in the natural.

The One who made that arrangement had a purpose for your time on earth, and that is why it happened precisely at the time and place it did—giving you a defined lifetime in which to achieve His purpose for you. When you know this, you will have so much peace; and, when you are carrying out His purpose for you, it will bring you so much joy and fulfilment.

Know Yourself Very Well

Many people have become "successful" by the standards of this world, largely because they have acquired material things or achieved fame; but they do not have inner peace or fulfilment. They feel that "something is missing" in their lives. Some of these people have committed suicide and shocked the world which thought they were so successful and so worth emulating. But they were not fulfilled because they did not know their purpose; they were going without direction through life.

If you do not know what your purpose in life is, I suggest that you find some resources to get you going. Fortunately, there is a lot written on this subject, and so you can find some good materials to help. Rick Warren's book, *The Purpose-Driven Life*, is a leader on this subject. My own book, *The Power of Two* (2008) contains some useful insights too.

In sum, your purpose is usually connected with the talents and gifts your Creator gave you, even before you were birthed. In many cases, these talents and gifts would have been apparent even at a tender age. As you grow, it becomes clear that these talents and gifts—which are already inside you—are leading you in certain directions. Therein lies your purpose. An overarching purpose may have sub-purposes or assignments connected with it; but they are all leading in the same direction.

Some people think having a purpose means that you have to be a pastor, evangelist, worship leader or deacon, or that you have to work in a church in some capacity.

This may be so for some, but it is not necessarily the case for everyone. Not everyone is called to be pastor, prophet, apostle, evangelist, deacon or church worker. If that is not your calling and you force your way into it (because it gives you status and looks good in public), you will be struggling (with lots of disappointments and setbacks) and you will not even obtain fulfilment.

Once you know your purpose, you will know the way to your destiny. You will have focus in life. You will know that you can do what your Creator has chosen you to do—and this may have nothing to do with becoming a pastor, prophet, apostle, evangelist, and so on. You simply have to serve your Creator where He wants you to be and do what He wants you to do.

Some people have been put on this earth to serve as engineers, doctors, lawyers, business people, teachers or financial advisers, according to God's plan for them. They can all serve just where they have been put, and they do not have to abandon their professions to become pastors or prophets or evangelists. These days, it is common to talk of a person's "ministry"; it may be another way of talking of the person's calling or purpose in life.

Once you find your purpose, it will come with provision. The One who gave you the purpose will make available to you what you need to carry out that purpose. Associated with this is that your Creator will bring to you helpers—people who will help you achieve your purpose in life, because He did not intend that you do it the hard way, all alone.

You should bear in mind that the purpose given to you is actually your Creator's; He has simply appointed you to fulfill an aspect of it. Yours is significant, but it is only a small part of His own big picture, His grand vision.

People who do not know their purpose in life tend to jump on the bandwagon; they just follow the crowd and grab onto any fad or new trend that comes along. Some time ago, I was speaking to somebody and he told me that, with my qualifications and background, it would be better for me to resign from my position with the United Nations and go back home, where I could easily rise to be the Attorney-General or Minister of Justice.

For a while, I kept quiet, but this guy would not back off. He kept yapping on. So, finally, I asked him: "Do you know your purpose in life?" He was taken aback. I told him that, as for me, I knew why I was put on earth, and so I did not have to waste my time guessing what would be good for me.

I told him that becoming the Attorney-General or Minister of Justice of a country, or for that matter becoming a politician, was not my purpose in life and so I did not have to imitate others or follow the crowd. That shut him up.

Many people have been drawn into high-flying careers because of the prestige associated with certain lines of work or because they got good grades in school, which automatically led them into those careers. For others, they were encouraged or even pressured by their parents to go into particular professions because that was the wish of the parents or because the family had for generations pursued that profession. In such cases, no consideration was given at all to the person's purpose. The parents were more interested in their family history or prestige than in finding out the Creator's purpose for their offspring.

On this point, we can compare Archbishop Desmond Tutu with the late Nelson Mandela. They worked together to bring down apartheid in South Africa; they were both activists, but from different angles. Archbishop Desmond Tutu was and still remains a priest—that is his calling, his purpose in life. Nelson Mandela, on the other hand, was chosen to lead his people out of bondage, using talents and gifts which his Creator put in him from the outset. He was not called to be a pastor or evangelist, and he did not go into the pulpit to preach sermons.

Both Archbishop Tutu and Nelson Mandela understood their particular purpose in life; they collaborated at some stage but from different perspectives. That did not mean that they had the same purpose or calling in life. We can find many examples like this in every country, and this is the case not only for high-profile people; the same applies to "ordinary" people.

Everyone has a purpose in this life; no one is on this earth to go through the motions or to be a bystander. On the contrary, everyone has a specific purpose, a particular role to play. No one is left out, unless they choose to remain ignorant by not discovering their purpose—or choose not to carry it out when they have discovered it.

Conclusion

Before you think of looking for a life partner, you should make sure that you are ready for a relationship. You should examine all aspects of your life in this regard. You should be aware of your strengths and weaknesses. Where you have identified areas which call for improvement or change, you should take steps to do so.

In particular, it is important to know your purpose in life and make sure that you are working on it. It is also advisable to educate yourself on relationships, especially life partnerships. Do not take things for granted and think that you can do it. You will come to realize that it requires a lot of effort to have a successful and happy relationship, and so the hard work should start now. You can begin by reading books like this very one.

Key Points to Remember

1. Nobody is on this earth by chance or coincidence; everyone has a purpose in life.
2. It is critical to know one's purpose in life.
3. Carrying out your purpose will serve as a compass in leading you to achieve your destiny.
4. Accomplishing your purpose will bring you inner peace, joy and fulfilment.
5. No matter how successful you might appear to the world, if you do not know your purpose or you do not carry it out, you would have wasted your time on this earth.

Questions to Ponder

i. Do you know your purpose in life?

ii. If so, what steps are you taking to achieve it?

iii. If not, what are you doing about it?

iv. Does your current job allow you to carry out your purpose? Or is your job such that you can only carry out your purpose "on the sidelines"? If the latter description fits your situation, what are you doing or planning to do about it?

PART B

COMMENCING THE SEARCH

Chapter 4

Do You Really Have to Start a Relationship Now?

Healthy relationships should always begin at the spiritual and intellectual levels—the levels of purpose, motivation, interests, dreams, and personality.

Myles Munroe

Why now?

So you want to get married because your friends are doing so? You should consider carefully whether this is enough reason for you to tie the knot at this point of your life. Those friends of yours may have their own reasons for marrying, and their situations may be different from yours. So you should not be a copycat or jump on the bandwagon, just because it may seem cool to others. Nor should you yield to peer pressure from anybody.

It is good for you to support your friends by attending their weddings or helping in some other way. But this does not mean that you also have to get married now. I hope those friends of yours have carefully weighed the pros and cons before deciding to get married. I hope they did not yield to pressure from their peers or from parents who are more concerned about having grandchildren than about whether their children are ready for marriage. I also hope your friends have laid solid foundations for their marriages before they started building on them.

Give it more careful consideration

Choosing a life partner is one of the most crucial decisions one can ever make. This is because it will lead to marriage, which is meant to be forever. Most things in life have an expiry date, written or unwritten. For example, at some point in time, you will retire from your job. Although, these days, there is no mandatory retirement for some jobs in some countries—an example is an academic position with tenure—the current norm is that most jobs do come with a stipulated retirement age.

The reality is that sooner or later you will get to the point when your body starts telling you to take a backseat and relax or retire altogether, even if by law you don't have to. This is the reality with most things in life—they do have an expiry date. The United Nations post that I hold now is meant to be continuing but, at some stage, I would have to retire and go home.

With relationships, some people will come into your life for a short time, perhaps for the life span of a project. Others will come and stay for a while, perhaps to help you move to the next level, and then they will disappear. Yet others may be with you for a long time but they, too, eventually will go away or you may leave them behind. Such is the journey of life for each and every one of us.

Do You Really Have to Start a Relationship Now?

But marriage is an entirely different proposition; it is unique. When a person comes into your life for the purpose of marriage, that person has come to stay, forever—that is the intention, anyway. Therefore, before you commit yourself to marry anyone, you have to understand that this person, who will be your marriage partner, will remain with you till death. That is why such a person is referred to as a *life partner* and not, for example, a temporary partner or a live-in.

Even though you may be entering into it for the very first time, marriage is not meant to be a rehearsal or an experiment. It is perhaps the only event in life where you are expected to "get it right" at the first go and stay with it for the rest of your life.

This is especially so for Christian partners because, until a Christian man or woman actually ties the knot, he or she is not permitted to experiment with a number of things such as cohabiting or having sexual intimacy of any kind. Thus, in some respects, Christians are expected to enter green and raw (with no previous experience) into marriage, and yet get it right the very first time. This is very challenging to say the least.

This means that, if you get it right, it would be nice and enjoyable for the remainder of your life. On the other hand, if you get it wrong, your life could be miserable, also forever—you could be lurching from crisis to crisis. Just imagine a life like that; it could be, in fact, hell on earth. Therefore, before you make the decision to look for a life partner and enter into marriage, you must be sure that you are ready for a permanent partnership—

something you are meant to stay in for the rest of your life. If you are not sure about this, then hold it and reflect on your situation a bit more. If necessary, educate and re-educate yourself about it before you make that final decision.

There is nothing wrong with being single (at least for a while)

It is okay to remain single, at least for a while. Some people think that once you reach a certain age, your singlehood must necessarily come to an end. But there is no basis for such a view. You can remain single and be happy. Happiness and fulfilment will not necessarily come to you by entering into a relationship.

Tie your decision on this matter with your purpose in life

For me, the decisive factor as to whether to remain single or to get married is my purpose in life. We have already discussed how purpose acts like a compass in life, giving you focus and direction. We talked about how carrying out your purpose will lead you to achieve destiny and greatness. If you are going about life without knowing your purpose—or, having discovered it, you do not carry it out—you are wasting your time on this earth.

Hence, you have to consider whether you can carry out your purpose more effectively by remaining single or by entering into a relationship with another person. If you can achieve your purpose just as successfully either way, then you have to ask yourself which option would be better for you. This is a question you should answer by yourself, after a careful consideration of the whole of your circumstances. Once you are convinced that entering into a relationship with a view to marriage is the better option for you, then you can move on to the next step, which we will discuss in the following chapters of this book.

If, on the other hand, you come to the conclusion that you can better pursue your purpose in life by remaining single, then proceed as such—and don't let people decide for you or put pressure on you.[1] It is your life, and it is not a rehearsal. It is a one and final lifetime, so make the most of it. There are people who pursued and achieved their purposes in life whilst remaining single; the two who immediately come to mind are the Apostle Paul and our Lord Jesus Christ.

---

[1] *cf.* 1 Corinthians 7:8

KEY POINTS TO REMEMBER

1. Consider carefully if you really desire a relationship at this point in your life and why.

2. You should not go into it because your friends think it is cool or because of pressure from people such as your parents; after all, it is your life, not theirs.

3. Looking for a life partner is a critical step in a person's life, as it is intended to lead to marriage.

4. Marriage is not meant to be a rehearsal or an experiment; it is meant to be permanent.

5. You are expected to get it right at the very first go and to remain in it for as long as you and your partner are alive.

6. Many people will come in and go out of your life, each one for a period and a specific reason.

7. But the person who will be your wife or husband is meant to be with you for life.

8. Marriage has no expiry date and there is no provision for retirement from it.

QUESTIONS TO PONDER

i. Make a short list of people who have come into your life over the past few years, whether as personal or family friends, colleagues, teammates (such as in a sport or church group) or acquaintances.

ii. Where are they now?

DO YOU REALLY HAVE TO START A RELATIONSHIP NOW?

iii. What difference, if any, did each one make in your life?

iv. Were there any of them that you thought would still be with you today?

v. Were there any of them of the opposite sex that at some stage you thought you "liked" or were "falling in love with" or had some strong physical attraction to? Or you thought he or she could even end up being your life partner? Where are these people now?

vi. List five good reasons why you think you should end your singlehood now.

vii. If you want to get married, at what age would you consider it best to do so? Please explain.

CHAPTER 5

How to Go about Choosing a Life Partner Today

The most wonderful of all things in life, I believe, is the discovery of another human being with whom one's relationship has a growing depth, beauty, and joy as the years increase. This inner progressiveness of love between two human beings is a most marvelous thing, it cannot be found by looking for it or by passionately wishing for it. It is a sort of Divine accident.

Sir Hugh Walpole

Having made up your mind that you want to have a life partner, you now have to begin the search for a suitable person. "Where do I start?" is the question people often ask.

Seek God's will

Since you understand the importance of the spiritual aspect and you have a solid relationship with God, and moreover you know your purpose in life, you should seek God's will about your desire to enter into a lifelong partnership. Ask Him whether you should get married in the near future and how that partner you are going to find will help you to fulfil your purpose.

How to Go about Choosing a Life Partner Today

At the end of the day, what matters is achieving your destiny; and, if you can find a partner to help you do so, that is great. Also, don't forget that you are not walking alone, you are with your God. So, with an important decision such as this, you should have a conversation with Him first, and He will show you the way. He will tell you whether you should look for a partner and also when to do it. Such a decision is too important for you to think you can make all by yourself.

God speaks to us in different ways, the most common being the following:

- ✓ through His Word
- ✓ through His still, small voice
- ✓ through dreams and visions
- ✓ through His prophets

God speaks to me mostly through dreams, though He has also spoken to me on occasions through some of the other means. Therefore, I take my dreams seriously; I have a Dream Journal in which I record my dreams. God has also given me some anointing with dream interpretation. Thus, I am able to understand many of my dreams and also help others with interpretation of their dreams. When my dream is so complicated that I do not understand it, I seek interpretation from others. Through dreams, God has revealed many things to me in my life, including my career. It is helpful to know the way God speaks to you, so that you can pay attention accordingly.

Establishing a horizontal relationship with a common direction

You have established a Vertical Relationship with God; this is essentially a spiritual relationship. Now you want to establish a Horizontal Relationship with a partner-to-be—a relationship in the natural realm.

The Bible asks, "Can two people walk together without agreeing on the direction?" (*Amos 3:3, NLT*) If you are going to choose a life partner, then you have to look for one who will agree with your direction in life. By now, you should know your purpose and the direction it is taking you in life; this should help you in making your choice.

Your aim is to find someone who has laid the same (or similar) foundations that you yourself have already established. He or she must also understand spiritual matters and have thus laid a solid spiritual foundation. Moreover, this person must also have a vertical relationship with God and understand his or her purpose in life. In other words, the basic fundamentals should be the same for both of you.

If you come across someone who is physically attractive, and has other things going for him or her, but has not laid the same (or similar) foundations as yours or do not even understand them, you should delete that person's name from your memory. It is a no-go for you. Similarly, if you come across a person who has laid part of those foundations but has no idea about the other aspects, it is in your interest to give that one a miss.

For example, if you meet a person who has no understanding of the relevance of the spiritual realm or does not know what his or her purpose in life is, that one is not for you. This is because you would not be able to agree on a common purpose that would lead to fulfilling your destiny. Such a person could turn out to be a destiny wrecker.

I chose my wife because we have a common understanding of the matters I have been discussing here. We are both spiritual, understand our purpose in life, and agree on a common direction. For example, we share the Word of God together. We have even been guest ministers of the gospel together at a conference overseas.

Don't think you can change a person later

Some people say they don't mind accepting a life partner who has laid foundations in certain aspects but not in all the areas discussed in this book. They believe that, once they are married, they will be able to work gradually to change the other person.

This, however, would be a serious mistake to make, because you are not likely to succeed in changing the other person, and it will only bring untold challenges, frustrations and pain to your relationship.

You may succeed in changing some tiny little behaviors (quirks) in the other person, but you will not be able to make any radical changes in your partner (this will be discussed in greater depth in a later chapter). Only God can change a person.

When a person does not have the foundations to start with, how can you even think of putting up any building? The person you intend to change would stick to what he or she knows and believes in, and so your intentions and plans to pursue a common direction would not bear any lasting fruit.

Also do not forget that, whilst you are thinking of changing your partner, that very person would also be taking steps to change you. So, you are going to spend an enormous amount of time playing a game of cat-and-mouse in your home—you are secretly trying to change each other. It would be one problem after another, with no end in sight.

Instead of moving together in a common direction, you would be fighting at the crossroads about which route to take. Initially, the fighting might be subtle but, eventually, it would blow up into a full-scale battle. Instead of moving in a common direction, achieving a common purpose together, and fulfilling your destiny, you would find yourselves stuck at the crossroads, arguing and debating about which direction to take.

KEY POINTS TO REMEMBER

1. You should seek the will of God as to whether you should enter into a relationship now.
2. In establishing a horizontal relationship with a person, you should aim for somebody with a common purpose and a common direction.

3. If the person has not laid the same foundations as you, that person is not for you. You could be stuck at the crossroads.

4. Don't make the mistake of thinking that you can choose a person who has laid some foundations but not all of them or that you can change the person later.

5. It's a waste of time to choose a person who is not going to help you achieve your purpose or fulfill your destiny.

QUESTIONS TO PONDER

i. Do you know how God speaks to you?

ii. If so, have you found His will for you as to whether to start a relationship now?

iii. If you find a potential life partner who is caring, kind and generous, but who tells you he or she does not have time for spiritual matters, what would you do?

iv. You come across a likely life partner who tells you that, at your age, you still have plenty of time on your side, and so both of you should "enjoy life now" — meaning, going to discos and parties, living the high life, drinking and smoking. What would you do?

Chapter 6

Don't Go on a Wild Goose Chase

Chasing you is like chasing the wind, you're the one thing in life I know I will never have.

Anonymous

In their quest for a life partner, some people try to cut corners and do strange things. But when you have already established a vertical relationship with God and you are genuinely walking with Him, you have to remember that, in everything you do, you are not alone.

This is still the case even when you forget to specifically call on Him in a particular situation. It is the same with looking for a life partner and, as long as you bear this in mind, you can avoid going on a wild-goose chase.

However, not everyone keeps this basic principle in mind and, consequently, some people go through unnecessary heartaches and pains. They allow themselves to become desperate and, once they get to that point, they begin to do strange things. In this chapter, we will look at some of the more common schemes and stratagems that people come up with, in their quest for a life partner.

Looking for their missing rib

Some ladies say that, because Eve was made from Adam's rib, all ladies too must have come out of the ribs of men. Such men are destined to be their husbands and so they must locate them, wherever these men may be. Those who believe in this theory argue that the specific man who is their soul-mate must be out there somewhere, waiting for them. God meant them to be together and so, until such time that they actually meet and marry, the search must go on. So goes the argument.

The first question that must be asked about this is: do you know what your own rib looks like? Secondly, how are you going to tell whether a particular man is the person whose rib you came from? There must be something that has to draw you to a particular man in the first place, and by what criteria are you going to judge this?

Another aspect of this is that, if a lady is going out frantically searching for her missing rib, what is a man supposed to do? Just keep peering out and lifting up his shirt from time to time to display his ribs?

The lottery approach

Some people pray to God (or so they claim) and ask Him to let the first person they meet immediately after that prayer be their life partner. I understand that both men and women do this. They use this method when they have already met more than one person, but they are not sure which one to choose.

The question that has to be asked is: Is this really an answer to your prayer? Is the person who turns up immediately after the prayer somebody who has actually been sent by God, or did he or she just happen to be in the vicinity by coincidence? If it is God answering your prayer, shouldn't there be confirmation in one form or another?

This approach appears to be like playing the lottery, and it raises more questions than it answers. What if the person who turns up immediately after the prayer fails to meet the expectations of the one who made the prayer request? Worse, what if the one who turns up has no interest whatsoever in marrying the one who prayed? Who is to be blamed for it: God, or the person who prayed? The person who prayed, no doubt, would be thrown into confusion, and what would be his or her next move? Say another prayer like the one before?

The perfect guy (or gal)

Searching for the perfect guy or gal is simply a variation of the foregoing pursuits. One can search and search, but one might not find anybody who comes close to Mister or Miss Perfect. This is because perfect people do not exist. They might be in one's mind or imagination, and that is where they will remain. One could spend an endless amount of time, maybe even years or decades, and still not come close to finding the perfect partner. It is similar to searching for the missing rib.

Conclusion

One would only be going on a wild-goose chase if one were to adopt any of the three methods described above, or some other similar method. People who have not established a vertical relationship with God in the first place or who are going through life without knowing their purpose are likely to find themselves listless. Without an anchor or direction in life, they may come to the point where they become willing to try anything.

These people may resort to the lottery approach, or they may search for their missing rib or for Mister or Miss Perfect. These are but examples of going on a wild-goose chase, and they are bound to result in heartaches, pain and frustration. God's timing is the best, but this often requires a lot of waiting.

In the following chapter, I will show you a more meaningful approach to finding a life partner.

Key Points to Remember

1. Searching for a life partner can be like a wild-goose chase if one is not careful.

2. There is no Mister or Miss Perfect out there.

3. There is no missing rib out there for you to find.

4. Remain focused on your relationship with God and the purpose God has given you, and you will find your life partner in due course.

Questions to Ponder

i. Did you previously know about the missing rib approach?

ii. What other ideas or methods have you heard about finding a life partner?

iii. Did you ever find yourself in a situation where you had to choose between two or more potential life partners? How did you resolve it?

iv. Do you believe it is possible to find Mister or Miss Perfect? If so, what criteria would you use?

CHAPTER 7

Qualities to Look for and How to Go about It

Ask, and it will be given to you; seek, and you will find; knock, and it will be opened to you.

Matthew 7:7

Everyone likes a person who is attractive and appealing to the eye. There is no exception to this; I have never come across a man or woman looking for an ugly person to marry. In their search for a life partner, men invariably start with women they find attractive.

Almost all ladies, too, want men who are tall—and rich. Some of them additionally want men who are famous or at least well-known. Men who are not gifted with height seem to have a distinct disadvantage in this regard. (But I know that they tend to have a solid center of gravity, and they are stable. Also, some of them are rich, anyway!)

In short, men like beautiful women, and women like handsome men. And it is not good enough that they consider their prospective partner to be attractive. He or she must be someone their friends will admire too; they have this need for endorsement or affirmation from the people in their lives. This is particularly so with ladies.

They like to obtain positive affirmation from their friends that the man pursuing them is really seen as handsome, not only by the lady concerned, but also by her friends. This is also the case with men, but to a lesser degree.

Having said this, it is also true that all of us have our own ideas about what we consider to be beautiful; at the end of the day, beauty is in the eye of the beholder, and that is all that really matters. This means that the obvious starting point in looking for a life partner has to be how you see the other person: do you like his or her looks?

Beauty might be the starting point, but one has to go beyond the surface to find out the true qualities of the person. The Bible has warned us that "Charm is deceptive, and beauty evaporates, but a woman who has the fear of the LORD should be praised" (*Proverbs 31:30, GW*). There is also a book by Judge Judy Sheindlin with a title that says it all: *Beauty Fades, Dumb Is Forever: The Making of a Happy Woman*. The point is that external beauty will eventually fade. Hence, if you go for a woman who is beautiful but dumb, one day you will end up with double jeopardy—faded beauty, and still not smart!

The same applies to a good-looking but foolish or wayward man. For example, if he is into drugs, porn or other vices, and you become so besotted with him that you overlook his weaknesses and go ahead and marry him—you are going to end up with a handsome man who is always stoned, shirks his responsibilities, and doesn't want to work. Worse, he could be abusing you.

These days, even people with average looks can make themselves look good with make-up, proper grooming, and flattering attire and accessories. Put another way, anyone who has the means can look impressive, even without natural good looks. It's all about external beauty, how one looks on the outside.

On the other hand, there is inner beauty: what one really is inside; one's character and values. This is not something that can be bought with money or fabricated. It cannot be seen just by looking at a person, even at close range. Inner beauty has to be revealed; or, where it is actively concealed, it has to be exposed gradually.

Combine inner beauty with external beauty

In searching for a life partner, you should look not just for external but also inner beauty, giving the latter dominant consideration. External beauty will attract you to a potential partner, but you should then look for inner beauty in the person.

Unlike external beauty, inner beauty is not easily discerned just by looking at someone; you will need to get to know the person well. You can tell whether someone possesses external beauty the first time you meet him or her. Sometimes, your eyes may play games with you, and so you may need to see the person again for confirmation. However, in most cases, external beauty is noticeable at first glance. A subsequent meeting will only serve to confirm that your eyes are not playing tricks on you.

However, you cannot detect inner beauty with your eyes, no matter how many times you look at a person. This is because inner beauty is hidden and needs to be brought out. What you need to look for in a life partner is a lovely personality. Therefore, if there is no inner beauty, don't waste your time on the person. Stand strong and resist the temptation being thrown your way by someone who is attractive on the outside but ugly or rotten on the inside. Give the person a miss; this one is not for you.

An instructive example is Delilah in the Bible. She looked stunning; Samson found her so attractive that he could not control himself. But Delilah was evil inside, and she betrayed Samson more than once, even to his death.[2]

If it is only external beauty you are looking for (and some people do make that mistake), your search need not take long. You will find good-looking men and women everywhere. Even if you set very high standards, believe me, you will find them; there are head turners in all walks of life. But, if you desire inner beauty as well (as this book is advocating), you will need to exercise patience.

Draw up a checklist of the qualities you desire

Make a checklist of the character traits that you really want in a partner, and take it to God in prayer, to start with. This is a private and confidential list which no one will ever see, so pour out all that is within you regarding the qualities you desire in your life partner.

---

[2] *cf.* Book of Judges, chapters 13-16

Qualities to Look for and How to Go about It

Do not take any quality for granted or consider it to be minor or less important. In this case, everything is important. This is a once-in-a-lifetime decision, so take your time; reflect, and reflect some more, and then make out your checklist. You will need days to do this.

Your checklist will achieve three objectives. First, it will enable you to form clearly in your mind what it is you are really after. When you speak to people and ask them what they are looking for, often you will find that—apart from one or two things they are sure of—they have not seriously thought about it. They just assume that, once they find those one or two qualities, the rest will come with them. But this is a mistake; it does not actually work that way.

Then there are those who tell you that they know what they are looking for and, when they come across it, they will somehow "know". But this is not a good way to go about it. The truth is that those who adopt this approach are not yet sure of what they want; they are just hoping someone "nice" will come along. But what is "nice"? If you do not have any criteria to assess "niceness", you will end up looking at only a person's external beauty.

To go through life, saying that you know what you want and that when you see it you will recognize it, means that you have actually not thought the matter through. And, though you may be looking, you are not really sure what you are looking for. You can be blown in any direction by the wind.

The second objective behind the checklist is to present a specific case to God. When you pray, you pray a specific prayer, asking God to help you locate a person with specific attributes. God can see the whole world and so, once you have put your checklist to Him, He will begin to locate a person who fits your requirements, and He will lead you to that person. This is something you cannot do as a human being, since you are confined by limitations of time and space. But God has no such limitations; He can see in the spirit who it is who fits your requirements, and He can join you in achieving your purpose.

However, you have to bear in mind that, if you put unrealistic or scripturally unacceptable requirements on your checklist, God will not grant those. So your checklist has to conform to God's own principles as well. In reality, you should not have trouble with this if you are already walking and communing with Him daily and you know His principles.

The third purpose of the checklist is to help guide you when you meet people. As and when you meet someone you like, filter him or her through your checklist. You can then tell if this person meets your criteria. Earlier, we talked about going beyond external beauty; this means that you will need to get close to the person, at least for a while, to ascertain if he or she possesses the inner beauty you are looking for. Another way of putting it is that you should not settle for someone simply because you have "fallen in love at first sight" with him or her. If you do, it means you are not following your own checklist; you are only looking at the person's external beauty.

Contents of the inner beauty checklist

This is entirely up to each person, as what appeals to one person may not necessarily be a strong factor for another. However, you should be guided by the solid foundations which you have already laid and the realization that you are looking for someone with whom you can fulfil your destiny. You are not just looking for someone "nice" to be your companion or mate. Rather, you are looking for somebody with whom you can agree on a common direction.

People who have not laid the type of foundations we talked about earlier and who do not understand their purpose in life are most likely to come up with a list which is entirely different from yours. The factors which will be dominant on their minds will be different from yours.

The focus is not on what you see with your eyes

In drawing up your checklist, don't be distracted by things like height, weight, shape or colour. These are features which you can see or tell, and so you do not need to make a checklist of them. I am not saying that they are not important, of course they are. But they belong in your external beauty checklist.

External beauty is not only about facial looks but other attributes like shape, colour and height as well. Similarly, considerations like the education and background of a person could be lumped together under this category—though, strictly speaking, they should be on their own.

Another factor is age. This can be a tricky one, as it is not always easy to tell a person's age. Some people are so attractive that they look much younger than they actually are. (The opposite may also be true in many cases.) Nevertheless, it is not difficult to find out, and so it should be categorized under the list of external beauty attributes.

The age of the partner-to-be may not be important to some; but it is for others. I have heard it said that age is just a number, but in many cases it does give some indication of one's maturity level. (Maturity is listed below as one of the qualities you might want to include in your inner beauty checklist). Ideally, the age gap should not be too wide. Or, put another way, the partners should not come from different eras, so to speak.

Graca Machel, former first lady of Mozambique, got married to President Nelson Mandela when she was fifty-two years old and he was eighty—thus becoming the first and only woman to be first lady of two different countries. She was initially reluctant to marry him but later gave in, and they remained inseparable until the death of Nelson Mandela in 2013. He was reported to have said that she made him "bloom like a flower".

Your inner beauty checklist

To get you started on your checklist, here are some examples of qualities to look for in a life partner:

- ✓ God-fearing
- ✓ Spiritual—prays, fasts, etc.
- ✓ Generous/kind—gives to charity, the poor and needy

- ✓ Caring and considerate
- ✓ Has integrity and good character
- ✓ Mature
- ✓ Has the same sense of humor as you—so that you can laugh together
- ✓ Dignified and respectful
- ✓ Humble—not proud or arrogant
- ✓ Believes in purity, sexually and morally

At the risk of repetition, it should be emphasized that, in drawing up this list, you are not merely looking for someone who would be compatible with you. Rather, you are looking for someone with whom you can agree on a common direction, with a view to fulfilling your purpose and achieving your destiny.

Such an approach may limit your pool, but this is good because you will focus only on the right people. This is what will make your checklist unique; it will be your own and not like everyone else's.

Stand out from the crowd

You want to meet the right person so that you can start a relationship and get married? You are not alone; there are many people in the same boat as you. As a matter of fact, it is crowded out there for both males and females. Dating sites (Christian and others) are saturated with people seeking life partners, but the going is tough. So you have to take steps to stand out from the crowd.

Starting with the external beauty aspect, make sure you always look good—nothing extravagant, but on the other hand don't look so tired, as if you are carrying the weight of the world on your individual shoulders.

If your Creator did not give you striking good looks, you can make up for it with a little investment in nice clothes and good deportment. Be consistent in taking care of your looks, throughout the week and on weekends, wherever you go. You don't know where or when the right person will turn up. Even if you are blessed with natural good looks, you need to maintain them so that you will look good all the time.

Always have an easy disposition towards others: pleasant smile, warm outlook, good sense of humor, positive attitude and choice of words, confidence in yourself. Generally speaking, what you give out is what you will get back: if you are friendly to people, they will be friendly in return; if you are kind and generous, you will get that in return. On the other hand, if you are obnoxious and difficult, people are likely to respond in like manner towards you.

Where inner beauty is concerned, be yourself. Remain steadfast with God, and follow His principles. Remember the foundations which you have already laid, and build on them; they are the fundamentals, so stick to them.

Remember at all times to walk by faith and not by sight, and to exercise that faith in your quest for a relationship. The Bible teaches us that we can call things into being by faith and we should not be discouraged by what we see happening around us.[3] We also know that delay does not necessarily mean denial; God's timing is always the best.

One of the most powerful principles I have learnt in life is that of giving—being generous and kind to others. This does not necessarily refer to paying tithes and giving offerings to your church. Rather, it means having a generous spirit and giving help to those who genuinely need it.

Yes, giving away money. But it can also mean giving other things which are precious to you; giving to people who need those things but are helpless and don't have them; and, more importantly, giving to those who have no way of repaying you. I have learnt that giving brings lots of blessings and rewards. If you make it part of your life, it will benefit you tremendously.

Go for potential

Men and women who are looking for life partners tend to go for people who are "ripe" for the picking. This may partly explain why it takes some people so long to find the "right one". This is especially true for some ladies. They want a man who has already made it in life; he must be rich and famous or have in some other way "arrived", with a nice house, nice car, good job, good education, high status and all the trimmings of success.

---

[3] *cf.* Mark 11:22-24; Romans 4:17

This happened with the lady I first had my eyes on. Her family did not warm up to me, and I later learnt that they did not think I was suitable—because, according to them, I had only one pair of trousers and one pair of shoes. I had just graduated from law school with a good class—I had a future. But, at the time, I had only one nice pair of trousers and shoes, and so I reserved them for important occasions. I had not realized that I was turning up at the lady's place in the same set of trousers and shoes—and maybe shirt too. (Even if I had realized, I might not have had a choice!) I was not considered worthy at the time.

Today, my wardrobes are full; I have everything in abundance, and I can basically afford anything I want. My situation today is so vastly different from many years ago, when I had just graduated from university. I have heard similar stories from other people. The point I want to make is that, in choosing a life partner, we should not dwell on what he or she is today. Circumstances can change in life, and so it is better to have someone you can grow with.

Bearing in mind that you are searching for a lifelong partner, you should look at the potential in the person—where he or she is likely to be in the coming years. The focus should not only be on the material aspect but, equally important, on other areas of life as well—spiritual, emotional, psychological, and so on. To put it another way, look for somebody you can grow and mature with; not someone whose life you cannot contribute to, nor him or her to yours.

Qualities to Look for and How to Go about It

For example, in the workplace, some people look down on others who are holding low-level positions. But these colleagues who are now at the bottom may be on the way up. Perhaps, in ten years, they will be right at the top or up there in the top echelon. The same goes for all other areas of life; so you should not reject anyone because today they are in a lowly place. We are all on a journey.

I have heard of ladies who rejected men because they deemed them to be "unsuitable" at the time the men approached them—only to go searching for those same men years later, because the men had made big leaps in life. But they had left it too late, as the men were no longer available—or they have had other ideas since then.

So in conclusion, go for potential. If you find somebody who is "ripe" and meets your requirements on inner and external beauty, well and good. But don't spend endless amounts of time searching for such a person.

There is no perfect partner out there. You can make your partner-to-be the one you want by growing together, building on the solid foundations you have both laid.

KEY POINTS TO REMEMBER

1. It's not a good idea to fall in love at first sight.
2. Combine external beauty with inner beauty.
3. Your inner beauty checklist should be in alignment with the foundations you have already laid and should point you to a person who will help you fulfill your purpose and achieve your destiny.
4. Ensure that you yourself stand out from the crowd and not be lost in it.
5. Go for someone with potential, and not necessarily one who is "ripe for the picking". Find someone you can grow with, whose life you can add value to.

QUESTIONS TO PONDER

i. Did you ever come across someone you were really interested in, but she or he showed no interest in you at all? What do you think was the explanation? Where is the person now?

ii. Do you take steps to ensure that, whatever setting you are in, you present yourself in the best way possible?

iii. Did you ever say no to somebody who was interested in you because you considered that person to be "not your type"? Please explain.

iv. In view of what you have learnt so far in this book, do you consider yourself ready to look for a life partner, or you would like some more time to consider the matter a bit further?

PART C

GETTING TO KNOW YOUR PARTNER

CHAPTER 8

Commencing an Exploratory Friendship

There are three things that amaze me—no, four things that I don't understand: how an eagle glides through the sky, how a snake slithers on a rock, how a ship navigates the ocean, how a man loves a woman.

Proverbs 30:18-19, NLT

At last, you have found somebody! She is so beautiful. Or, he is such a handsome guy. You are happy with the height, shape, looks, education, background, everything. Your heart begins to melt when you see him or her, or when you look at that photo. Just seems like the type you have been dreaming about. Now, he—or she—is here, in the flesh! Your next move is to get to know this person better, to ascertain if he or she possesses the inner beauty you are looking for.

You need to make a thorough assessment and get the full picture yourself. Hence, it is necessary to get close to the person—there is no other way. You cannot even rely on family members to do this for you, unless you are prepared to take their word for it. You should keep in mind that the other person would also like to get to know you well and not just rely on the word of third parties.

For this purpose, the two of you need to become close friends. In some cases, it may be a long-distance friendship by phone or email. Making contact this way may actually not be that difficult. The norm, however, is to meet in person. On the surface, this may seem straightforward. But, in practice, it could be the most challenging move you would ever make—because, to-date, you are the only one harbouring feelings for the other person.

Indeed, you might even think you are falling in love with him or her. But you have no idea what the other person actually thinks or feels about you. Maybe, he also feels good about you. Or, maybe, she has not even noticed you. You may not even be on her emotional radar screen.

If you are in a close setting (such as in the same workplace or organization) and you see each other regularly or from time to time, it will help. Similarly, being in the same church or fellowship group is an advantage. Nevertheless, it does not change the fact that making this first move can be very daunting.

Men, what should be your strategy? When do you approach the girl of your dreams, and what are the first words that should come out of your mouth? In emotional matters, timing is very important, especially so with this very kind of first approach. You should plan to approach her when she is likely to be in a good mood, not when she is exhausted from work or some other activities and just wants to go home and rest. These are some of the important considerations when making your first move.

COMMENCING AN EXPLORATORY FRIENDSHIP

Most men (irrespective of their age) would have butterflies in their stomachs when they have to make this all-important first approach. But our Christian faith teaches us that this is one occasion when you have to first go into deep prayer (and maybe even fasting) for God to give you courage and favour—and wisdom as to when to make the move and the words to say to the lady when you approach her. Don't think that you can do this by yourself.

You don't need Dutch courage or some other kind of human bravado; that would not be enough. What you need is empowerment from God and the right words to say. Otherwise, you could make a total fool of yourself when you approach the lady. Also, some ladies do not make things easy for men. They do not want to be taken for granted, and so they would expect you to organize yourself well and say what you want to say clearly and confidently, without any assistance from them.

The question you have to ask yourself is: do you really like this person or are you "in love" with her, so much so that you want to start a friendship with her? How do you know the difference? If you cannot explain how you feel, you are not alone. Almost everyone goes through the same emotional experience. This is a bit of a mystery.

As *Proverbs 30:19* says, this is one of the great mysteries of life: how a man falls in love with a woman. Why this particular lady, what is it that has attracted you to her, out of all the ladies out there?

I would say that, at this stage, there is a strong element of infatuation involved. Even though one may use the word "love", it cannot truly be so at this point in time, because you are only looking at external beauty. You have not even reached the stage when you begin to know what this woman is truly like inside. Sure, you might know about some of her inner beauty attributes, if you are in the same church or same organization or if you know somebody who knows this person. But that is still not enough to be able to make a reasoned judgment.

Whether we like it or not, the lady is in a privileged position. No matter what the standing of the man is in society, it is up to the lady to say yes or no. If she says no, that is the end of the matter and a friendship cannot commence. (Some men might consider trying again later.)

Now, a word to the ladies: if you do not like the man or he does not meet the requirements on your checklist, please be gentle with him. You can simply say that you need time to think about it or give some other excuse (like you need to consult your parents first or your parents would not accept it).

Please don't put the man down. He has come to you in good faith, believing in his heart that he wants to start a friendship with you which may eventually end up in marriage. If you feel and think otherwise, that is fine; it is not unusual. But please do not belittle him or spread stories that you have rejected him. Please do not make the man feel small.

Commencing an Exploratory Friendship

Firstly, that is a terrible thing that you can do to a man. Secondly, you never know what the future might bring. This same man could one day be somebody significant in your life, such as in your workplace, and you may need him or even work under him. (You remember our earlier discussion about ladies who rejected men they considered to be unsuitable, only to go searching for them years later?) So, even if your answer is no, do it gently. No put-downs or degrading of the man.

Back to the men: when you are sure that God has given you the go-ahead and you make the initial contact and she responds positively, a friendship can then start. At this stage, you are just making contact and there is nothing more to it. You are starting a conversation and hoping that it will continue. You are just asking the lady out, and it is only between the two of you. You are hoping that the friendship will take off.

Some people may call it dating, but in my view you are simply laying the foundations for a friendship and you are not even sure if it will take off. You are engaging in what I call **Exploratory Friendship**. At this stage, the vibes that you exchange or the chemistry that develops will be a strong indication of whether the friendship should continue. It is more about how you feel toward each other.

During this stage, you can meet from time to time, speak on the phone, or communicate by way of text, email or letters. You may go for walks or for coffee or tea breaks. You may meet alone or in groups—the important thing is to find opportunities to get to know this person. It is of no use if you are not able to get close to the lady to observe her and especially talk to her. That would be a waste of time.

During this **Exploratory Friendship** stage, both the man and woman should observe certain basic rules:

- ✓ You are just friends—or trying to be—and so there is no talk of a relationship, let alone marriage;
- ✓ There is no commitment of any kind by either party;
- ✓ Romance and intimacy do not come into the picture;
- ✓ There should be no touching, kissing, holding of hands or anything intimate;
- ✓ You have to maintain your purity, and so there should be no sexual involvement with your friend.

At this stage, your family, friends, or persons in authority over you need not know about the nascent friendship. Just let matters take their natural course and allow the friendship to develop.

What is of key importance right now is to do a lot of talking, listening and observing. You know what you are looking for and so, armed with your checklist, make sure that this potential partner has the qualities you want.

COMMENCING AN EXPLORATORY FRIENDSHIP

KEY POINTS TO REMEMBER

1. When you have found a person who seems to be a potential partner, prepare for the first encounter. Pray to God for favour, courage and blessings. Ask Him to give you the right words to say.

2. If the woman does not like the man, she should tell him "no" in a gentle manner, not put the man down.

3. When a friendship commences, it is only an exploratory friendship; it is not yet a relationship and so there is no commitment on either side.

4. Nevertheless, there are some basic rules which must apply.

5. The friendship at this stage may be secret and persons in authority over the would-be partners need not know about it.

QUESTIONS TO PONDER

i. What are the various ways in which you (a man) can make your first approach to a lady to express an interest in her?

ii. Can you think of any special words to use? Would you first write down what you would say and memorize it?

iii. How would you react if the lady is not interested? Would you consider trying again at a later date? How many times would you be prepared to do this?

iv. You are a lady and you have been approached by a man who at first blush seems okay. How would you react? What would you say?

v. You are a lady and you have been approached by a man, but you are not interested at all. How would you handle the situation? Would you chase him away and warn him never to come near you again?

vi. Would you consider being involved in two exploratory friendships at the same time? If yes, why? If no, why not?

CHAPTER 9

Turning the Friendship into a Relationship

Satisfied needs produce fulfilled people, and fulfilled people are free to pursue and exercise their full potential as human beings. The primary goal, then, in any relationship should be the meeting of needs.

Myles Munroe

Do nothing out of selfish ambition or vain conceit. Rather, in humility value others above yourselves, not looking to your own interests but each of you to the interests of the others.

Philippians 2:3-4, NIV

You have been in the Exploratory Friendship stage for a while, and so far so good. You like your partner and enjoy being with him or her. You have been sticking to the rules of the game, but so far you have kept the friendship a secret (only a few friends know about it).

The next step is to develop the friendship. Take it a notch up, to what I call the **Getting to Know You Well Stage**; some people may call it courtship. You get to this stage only when you have been able to ascertain much of the inner beauty attributes of the person and you are convinced that he or she will make a good life partner.

At this stage, you have to formally express an interest in marriage. If he or she responds positively, you bring your friendship out into the open. Indeed, this is when you turn the friendship into a relationship.

You should bear in mind that, even though you may enjoy a good friendship with someone, it does not necessarily follow that you will suit each other as life partners. You are more likely to find out if this person is the one for you, as you get to know him or her well during this second stage.

Also, don't take it for granted that, since the lady likes you as a friend, she wants to be your wife; the same applies to a man becoming a husband. The two are different scenarios. Further, you should remember that your friend has his or her own checklist and is also trying to meet the requirements of *Amos 3:3*.

When I was looking for a marriage partner, I came across some ladies I liked as friends. I enjoyed their company, and I liked talking to them, having intellectual and spiritual conversations with them. But I did not want them as life partners because they lacked some of the key attributes on my inner beauty checklist.

So, having a good exploratory friendship with somebody does not necessarily guarantee that he or she would be interested in becoming your life partner—or would be a good one at that.

Some basic rules

During this stage, when you are bringing out your friendship into the open, some more rules would apply (in addition to the ones you have already been adhering to, during the Exploratory Friendship stage):

- ✓ Your friendship can no longer remain a secret. It has to come out and get approval. Somebody having authority over you must be informed and has to consent to the relationship. This may be your parent(s), pastor or some other recognized leader.

- ✓ The same goes for your prospective partner, who must seek similar endorsement from the authority figure(s) in his or her life.

- ✓ Your friendship is now a relationship, and so a commitment has to be made by both of you that you will work towards marriage.

- ✓ You cannot be involved in any other exploratory friendships—it is now just you and the person you intend to marry.

You should remember that you are still finding out more about the person you intend to be your life partner. During this second stage, you will be in an even better position to learn more about him or her. The guidelines on the following pages will help the two of you to develop your relationship further.

- ✓ You should be open to feedback. Earlier, we talked about knowing yourself very well to start with. Now that somebody is close to you, that person will be revealing to you things about yourself that you may not have known or understood (for example, some unusual mannerisms of yours). Take heed and make the necessary adjustments, not just to please your partner-to-be, but for your own self-improvement.

  Here is another example: if your friend says that you like talking but are not good at listening, don't get upset about it. Take note, examine yourself, and work on it, because this is an area which is a big problem in marriages. You are acting as a mirror for each other.

- ✓ Related to the foregoing is the importance of being yourself, of being honest. You should not pretend. During this stage, some people like to put on a good show—showing their best sides (in fact, exaggerating them), whilst trying to hide their weaknesses. However, this is not good. Courting couples should drop all pretence and let their true selves come out now, so that their would-be partners would be aware of what they are getting themselves into.

- ✓ Don't dwell on things which happened in the past. Instead, focus on the future. If, however, there are skeletons in your closet which are relevant to the future marriage, then you must disclose them.

Turning the Friendship into a Relationship

For example, if you have been married before or you have a love child somewhere, you must disclose this at the earliest opportunity. If you do not do so, it could lead to serious repercussions later on. Or, if the truth comes out, your integrity could be called into question.

I heard of a lady who failed to disclose to her husband-to-be that she had a love child. She left her child with her mother in the village and went to live in the city. Both she and her boyfriend were studying law then; they later got married and are now practising lawyers. They are not able to have a child of their own but, because the lady lied at the beginning, she cannot now tell her husband about this love child, who remains languishing in the village with the grandmother. The couple is now thinking of adopting.

On the other extreme end, some ladies will ask a man to provide a list of all the girl friends he had before. They say they do not want to be taken by surprise, if they were to meet any of them. But this is not wise, either for the man or the woman. The past is past, and it should not be brought up.

✓ Some people have had bad, hurtful experiences in friendships and relationships. Maybe you met somebody you thought was nice and sweet, and he or she made many promises to you; and later you found out that she was lying to you or he broke his promises. Consequently, the relationship did not progress to marriage.

Some relationships are known to have collapsed very close to the wedding date. I have even heard of cases where one of the partners did not turn up for the wedding. No doubt, these are very painful experiences, and some people find it hard to get over them and move on with their lives.

There are people who may have had more than one such painful experience and, as a result, they have formed a very negative opinion of the opposite sex. They allow those experiences to be in the foreground of their thinking and attitude. Thus, when they meet someone and enter into an exploratory friendship or a relationship, they are heavily influenced by those past experiences.

Some of them even like to talk about those past experiences all the time. But this is not a positive attitude; it can be quite toxic to a new relationship. Hence, dwelling on such experiences in particular—or on the past generally—is not healthy and should be avoided.

If you have had a nasty experience and it is still bothering you, it probably indicates that you have not forgiven whoever has wronged you and you are not ready for a new relationship. You need to forgive and forget, so that you can move on with your life.

You should ask God to help you with this. Once you have forgiven the person, God too will forgive you and wipe the slate clean for you. You must not burden a new relationship with things that happened in the past.

Turning the Friendship into a Relationship

Furthermore, if you know you have committed sins in the past, ask God for forgiveness. Ask Him to release you from that bondage, so that you can be free to move on with your life.

- ✓ Be careful of some friends. Often, when we meet someone we think we are in love with, the first thing we do is tell our friends—in particular those we consider to be our best friends. This is especially so with ladies; they do so to get affirmation and encouragement from their friends. But be careful of spoilers; not all those we consider our friends are truly so at heart.

Some friends are alright with you when you are still in the Exploratory Friendship stage; but, as soon as you tell them that your partner is interested in marrying you, their attitude towards you may change. They become envious or jealous of you, because you will have a change of status and leave them behind; or they may even be interested in your potential partner themselves, once they learn a little bit more about him or her. Some may even be plotting to push you out and take your intending partner.

So, be on your guard and keep some things to yourself; keep some friends out of it altogether, before they wreck things for you. One of the ploys people use these days is to tell you that they saw something negative in a dream about the person you are intending to marry. Others will come to you and say that they have received a negative prophecy regarding the person you have found.

Please be careful of such people. Did they share the dream or prophecy with you previously? Or is it because you told them you have found a potential life partner? Why did they not get the dream or prophecy before? More importantly, if God had something to tell you, He would have done so directly, or at any rate confirmed it with you. You remember our earlier discussion on how God speaks to people?

- ✓ Play together, pray together, and fast together; do as many things as possible together.

- ✓ Attend marriage seminars, workshops and conferences that will help prepare you for married life. These days, many churches conduct marriage preparation classes; take advantage of them.

- ✓ Look out for books, videos and other helpful resources on relationships and marriage, and share them with your partner-to-be.

- ✓ Pay particular attention to how your partner communicates. Is he straightforward? Does she like to go round about before making a point? Does he allow interactive communication? Does she like to do all the talking and expect you to just listen?

- ✓ Study your partner's likes and dislikes; look out for his or her favorite foods, restaurants, outdoor or indoor activities, colours (not only for clothes but generally). Does your partner-to-be like going for walks to the beach or park? Does he or she enjoy movies or videos and, if so, which types—romances, mysteries, thrillers?

Turning the Friendship into a Relationship

- ✓ Does your intending partner like to go out with his or her friends (of the same sex) or does he or she prefer going out with you? As the relationship develops, pay attention to any changes in this regard—for example, at the start of the friendship, your partner might have been more interested in being with his or her friends rather than you, but with time you notice the reverse happening. Or vice versa.

- ✓ Learn as much as you can about each other and your families. Meet each other's parents. The more you know about each other and your respective families, the better. The knowledge you gain will prepare you better for the marriage itself—so that, once you get into it, there should not be too many surprises.

- ✓ Don't try to change your partner. As you learn more about this person, you will have to decide if this is what you really want. If yes, then you have to accept your partner-to-be the way he or she is. (It might be a good idea if you think you should adjust by changing some things about yourself.) But don't make any attempt to change your partner or decide that you will proceed to change him or her after the marriage. It would not work, and you would be bringing upon yourself much unwarranted pain and frustration.

    If you desire anything to be changed in your partner, pray to God for it. (At the same time, you can gently encourage your partner to change at his or her own pace).

- ✓ Don't shift your focus entirely from God to your partner. You have already established a vertical relationship with God, and so has your partner-to-be. Both of you are now trying to establish a horizontal relationship between yourselves—and also trying to meet the requirements of *Amos 3:3* by having a common direction.

God has to remain at the centre of the relationship you are trying to establish with your partner-to-be. You cannot now shift the focus (which you had on God from the start) to your partner. Rather, your objective should be to have God at the centre of the new-found relationship as it develops and matures.

I have heard people say that marriage should be like an equilateral triangle, with God at the apex. However, I have a different view. I do not think that an equilateral triangle is an appropriate analogy—because, in an equilateral triangle, all three sides are equal. But neither of you can be equal to God.

Rather, my teaching in this book is that you should end up forming a reinforced Cross, with the two vertical relationships—already in existence between God and each partner—being subsumed into one; and this vertical relationship is now reinforced over the horizontal relationship between the partners. It then becomes a reinforced Cross, with Jesus being the central pillar.

Turning the Friendship into a Relationship

- ✓ Don't cohabit. In some countries, cohabiting is lawful; for example, in USA, UK, Australia and South Africa, the law recognizes the unwed partners as husband and wife in almost all respects. But cohabitation is definitely contrary to the tenets of the Christian faith. You should not move in with your partner-to-be when you are not yet married.

- ✓ This is the time to reveal your romantic side. Send flowers, nice little gifts, lovely cards with romantic messages. You can buy beautifully-designed cards that have been left blank for you to compose your own poems and messages. You can also send romantic text messages or emails. Send them often, but do not bombard him or her with them.

  If you can sing, serenade your partner with romantic songs—this applies to both partners. There are many love songs you can pick, and you can customize the lyrics, inserting his or her name where appropriate. There are also popular gospel songs that you can modify into love songs.

  Flowers, gifts, cards, messages and love songs will reveal your romantic side and also more of your inner beauty. This is important, in the absence of touching, kissing, fondling and other forms of intimacy which are "off limits" at this stage of your relationship. If you are unable to do anything to express your love, and you are always uptight, it may be concluded that you are boring and not romantic. Avoid getting such a label, it can be damaging; it is a relationship killer.

GETTING TO KNOW YOUR PARTNER

- ✓ Bear in mind that your primary aim in looking for a partner is to find someone with whom you can fulfill your purpose in life and attain your destiny.

- ✓ Although you have made a commitment to each other, it is not an irreversible one during this **Getting to Know You Well** stage. If you find out that some things are not what you thought they were, you should feel free to withdraw from the relationship. But a decision to withdraw cannot be made on flimsy grounds. You have made a commitment with God as your witness, and you would have invested a lot of emotional and other capital into the relationship.

    I would like to emphasize that a decision to end the relationship cannot be made lightly. Don't forget that God is in the center of this relationship. As *Galatians 6:7* says, "Do not be deceived, God is not mocked; for whatever a man sows, that he will also reap."

    There have to be sufficient grounds—fundamental reasons which go to the heart of the relationship—to justify your breaking off with your partner: for example, if you discovered that your partner-to-be had lied to you about his or her background or about some other important matter, claiming to be someone he or she is not.

    Or, if your partner is already in a relationship with someone else, or has a love child somewhere and did not disclose this. Until you get to the altar and say, "I do", you are free to withdraw from the relationship. This applies to either partner.

Turning the Friendship into a Relationship

Finally, although I have already made the point that there should not be intimacy of any kind in your relationship, I want to emphasize it here, because this is an issue which troubles many young Christians today. One partner may exert pressure on the other to engage in intimacy. He or she might argue that, after all, you are going to get married and your parents (or pastors) have been informed of your commitment to each other; so there should not be any barrier to becoming intimate with each other. Such an idea should be resisted at all costs.

If the partner is truly a Christian and is interested in you and wants to abide by God's principles, then both of you have to maintain purity and stay away from sex until you get married. Other forms of intimacy such as kissing and fondling are also dangerous because they would arouse within you emotions you may not be able to control, and you could then end up having sex. This would be a serious sin before God, and it would ruin everything for you. Even if you go ahead and get married, you would have committed a cardinal sin, because you engaged in pre-marital sexual relations.

Sure, when you are in a relationship and getting to know your partner well, temptations will come; but you should resist them all. If you are a virgin or a virgin again, please maintain the life of purity until you actually get married. Some men put pressure on ladies by arguing that you cannot buy an expensive car without first taking it for a test drive. That is what they do in the world; but, in God's kingdom, the rules are different, and we must obey those rules.

I have also heard some men say that they would like to know whether the lady can get pregnant and have a child before they go ahead and marry her. Now, my reply would be that this is a matter for God and God only. Do you know how long it would take before this lady gets pregnant by you? Do you remember how long it took Sarah, Rebekah and Rachel (in the Bible) to get pregnant?

Hence, an argument that a lady must get pregnant before she can get married is not only against God's principles, it is also cruel as it can subject the lady to untold pain and suffering for years. A man who really loves a woman and wants to spend the rest of his life with her will not take such a stand.

Sometimes it is the lady who puts pressure on the man to engage in sexual relations, taunting him to demonstrate his manhood. If he refuses to do so, he may be labelled impotent. But premarital sex is forbidden by God. Indeed, the Bible teaches us to flee from any kind of sexual temptation and all its modern manifestations, including pornography, online sex, chat rooms, and so on. When Potiphar's wife tried to seduce Joseph to go to bed with her, he did no use persuasion or logic to overcome her. Instead, he ran away from her (*Genesis 39:11-12*). This is a very powerful example to us.

When your partner-to-be tries to lure or pressure you into premarital sex, you know it is time to move on. As a matter of fact, this is one of the justifiable grounds for withdrawing your commitment and abandoning the relationship. It is better to pull out rather than go against God's kingdom principles and sin against Him.

You have to realize that if a partner-to-be is prepared to violate this principle and obtain temporary pleasure by engaging in premarital sex, he or she would be prepared to violate any other rule we have discussed in this book. This could be the beginning of one or both of you going astray from your walk with God.

KEY POINTS TO REMEMBER

1. The relationship has progressed to the **Getting to Know You Well stage** (until then it had been an exploratory friendship).

2. A commitment to marriage has to be made during this stage.

3. The relationship cannot remain a secret, and so someone in authority over the partners-to-be must be informed about it.

4. The partners have to get closer to each other and really get to know each other well; this also includes getting to know each other's family well.

5. Intimacy of any kind is still not allowed. All the rules have to be obeyed.

6. Either partner may withdraw from the relationship if the other is not obeying the rules or wants to act outside godly principles. However, a decision to withdraw cannot be made on some flimsy ground— there has to be a solid basis.

QUESTIONS TO PONDER

i. What would you like to see in your friend, to make you cross over from the Exploratory Friendship stage to the Getting to Know You Well stage?

ii. How long do you think the first stage should take before you move to the second stage?

iii. What are some of the reasons which can justify a person withdrawing from a relationship?

iv. Have you ever been in a relationship which did not result in marriage? What happened?

v. What are the factors which will make you feel that you should tell your parents (or other persons having authority over you) that you have now met somebody you are willing to make a commitment to marry?

vi. What if your parents (or persons having authority over you) do not like the person and do not want you to continue with the relationship? What would you do?

vii. What if your parents insist that you have to marry someone from the same background, culture, race or country as you? What would be your response?

PART D

MAKING IT THROUGH THE COURTSHIP

CHAPTER 10

Learn Early to Give and Take

Love suffers long and is kind; love does not envy; love does not parade itself, is not puffed up; does not behave rudely, does not seek its own, is not provoked, thinks no evil; does not rejoice in iniquity, but rejoices in the truth; bears all things, believes all things, hopes all things, endures all things.

1 Corinthians 13: 4-7

One of the most important things you have to learn when you begin an **Exploratory Friendship** is to give and take. You have to start learning this early in the piece and keep at it as the friendship progresses to the **Getting to Know You Well stage**. This is one continuum which will operate throughout—from friendship, through relationship, to eventual marriage. If you begin early and take this seriously, you should be well-versed in it and it would have served you well by the time you get to the wedding.

You need to learn to give and take because the two of you are two different personalities coming from different backgrounds, with different experiences and expectations. Sure, there may be some similarities (hopefully, you have laid similar foundations) between you. In fact, those similarities might even have attracted you to each other in the first place. But there are bound to be differences too.

As independent human beings, you would each have your own thoughts, values, attitudes, expectations and desires, and also your own ways of doing things. Because of these differences, you are bound to have some disagreements or even disputes with your partner as you go along. For the friendship or relationship to work, you have to find solutions to such conflicts when they come.

Those who claim that they never have any disagreements or disputes in their relationship or marriage are, to put it mildly or diplomatically, species which (yes: *which*, not *who*!) belong to a different planet. They are trapped in their own fantasies and imaginations. Put any two human beings together, and there are bound to be disagreements and even disputes over some issue or other. This is especially so if they have to live together in the same home; the same goes for the workplace.

This does not mean that one partner is "good" and the other "bad". No, they are simply different, coming from different perspectives. You can even find this among siblings; this is how God made it to be. It is therefore important to know how to handle conflicts with loved ones. But, before we explore this subject, let us look at the immutable—what you cannot compromise on or change.

What you cannot compromise on

Certain principles are so fundamental that you cannot compromise on them. We have already looked at some of these; others will be discussed in more detail later in this book. Let us now recall some of these principles.

1. **You cannot compromise on your faith**

   Your faith is your foundation. It gives you your belief system. This is what makes you who you are; it gives you your identity. It is where you start from—your faith in God and your acceptance of His principles. So this is not something you can compromise on; it is one of the foundation pillars of your life. If you compromise on your faith in God, your life journey will take an entirely different course; the identity you started with will metamorphose into something else.

2. **You cannot compromise on Kingdom principles**

   Related to the first, or deriving from it, are the principles of the kingdom of God. These are set out in the Bible, and they have been guiding your life up to this point. They are fundamental to what you believe and the way you lead your life. You do not have the same lifestyle options as the world; rather, you are constrained and restrained by the principles of God's Kingdom. Indeed, you began your search for a life partner according to these very principles, and they have been guiding your search thus far.

   Our key verse, *Amos 3:3*, is one of those principles. Others are that you should not marry a person whose spiritual beliefs are different from yours, because there would be serious consequences in doing so. Further, you cannot cohabit or have pre-marital sex. These are fundamental Kingdom principles which cannot be compromised on.

3. **You cannot compromise on your purpose in life or your destiny**

   Your faith teaches you that God put you on this earth for a purpose connected with your destiny. You are not on this earth just to go through the motions and, when your time to die comes, you just go. God created you for a specific purpose in life. It is your duty to find out what that purpose is and do what is required of you; this will lead you to achieve your destiny.

   When you are all done and you depart this earth, you will meet your Creator and give an account of the time you had on this earth—in particular, whether you have achieved your purpose on earth. This is something you cannot compromise on; otherwise, your life on earth would have been a total waste of time. For example, Samson compromised on his purpose when he became entangled with Delilah. He lost his focus, and his end was disastrous.

4. **You cannot change a person.**

   No human being has what it takes to change another person. Only God can do so. Therefore, it is important for you to know that, if you are to get close to somebody and live with him or her, you have to accept the person as he or she is. Fundamentally, you cannot change the person.

You have to give and take on some things

Apart from your fundamental principles, you should learn to give and take on other issues. These are what I call optionals or variables—you have to be flexible on these. They can range over a whole gamut of matters.

Examples are whether you should both meet at one particular place or another, whether you should go for a walk on the beach, and, if so, which one. Or, when buying something, which colours you should select? All of us have our favourite colours; yours may be different from your friend's. Or, when watching TV together, which channel should you choose? Should you go to one supermarket or the other? The same applies to sporting and entertainment events.

Some of these matters may seem straightforward but, in practice, they do pose challenges. To avoid disputes, you have to learn to compromise. The closer you get to each other, the more such matters are likely to crop up, and you have to learn to give and take. If you insist on having your way all the time on every matter, you will reveal yourself to be rigid and difficult to get along with.

You have to learn to be flexible. By all means, stick to your convictions and do not compromise if the matter is of great moment to you, if it means a lot to you. If, however, the issue is only one of sentiment and not that significant, learn to give in.

Two important concepts which you need to have firmly in your vocabulary are "sacrifice" and "apologize". When you live alone, you may not face issues that call for a sacrifice. But, once you are involved in a friendship or relationship, the situation changes. Sometimes you have to make sacrifices for your friend's sake. For example, you may have to sacrifice some precious time to help your friend or accompany your partner to a place where he or she really wants to go.

Apologizing is something you have to learn to do too. It is difficult for many people to say "sorry", because their honour, ego or prestige may be at stake. But, once you are in a friendship or relationship, there will be times when you unwittingly offend your partner; for example, through the wrong or inappropriate choice of words, even though you may not have had a negative intention.

Once your friend raises the issue, and you realize your mistake and how he or she feels about it, you may have to apologize. If you are not used to saying sorry, then you have to learn to do so, because situations are bound to arise when you cannot avoid apologizing to your friend if you want the relationship to continue. It is always better to do ask for forgiveness at the earliest opportunity because, if you procrastinate, the problem may fester and get to the point where it becomes difficult to apologize without being seen to have capitulated.

In some cases, the give-and-take may entail both you and your friend meeting halfway—a true compromise. You will both have to give ground partially to each other so that the two of you can reach an amicable agreement. In other cases, the issue could be more challenging; that is, one of you has to give in altogether on certain matters. But it may be only on some occasions, not every time.

Learn Early to Give and Take

If you want to enjoy peace and make progress in your marriage, you may have to overlook certain matters at times. This is why it is important to learn to give and take at an early stage of the friendship. If you are not used to doing so, you will have to learn, and the best time to learn is at the Exploratory Friendship stage. This will give you ample time to get better at it, as the friendship turns into a relationship which may subsequently lead to marriage.

When you know how to give and take, you will have a happy marriage, because you will avoid unnecessary disputes over little things, such as where the toothpaste, comb or towel should be, whether in the bathroom or sitting room. But an attitude of give-and-take should not be one-sided. That is to say, I am not suggesting that you form the habit of compromising just to make your friend happy, if he or she is not prepared to do the same.

What I am teaching here applies to both sides of the friendship; that is why it is called "give and take". You give up some things and take some things. As already mentioned, in most cases this would involve meeting each other halfway. But, in a few cases, a compromise may call for you giving in altogether.

To put it another way, in many cases, you *negotiate*; you change your original stance and settle for less than what you had originally wished for. In the other category, you abandon your position and accept your friend's. You give in altogether in order to "buy peace". Be that as it may, this should not be one-sided; ensure that such occasions are the exception and not the norm.

In those marriages where couples claim that they have been married for many years but have never fought or had disputes, it is more likely than not that one partner is always giving in. One person would appear to be dominant, and he or she is having his or her way all the time. In such cases, there is no real negotiation, no give-and-take. Rather, the prevailing attitude is "Take it or leave it!"

Because one partner has been made to accept such a position from the beginning, there is always "peace" in the home. But this is a false peace because the person who is always having his or her way is actually dominating over the other partner and calling the shots all the time, while the other person has become subservient. This is not healthy as the subservient partner will become resentful. The marriage may seem peaceful until the resentment boils to the surface and everything explodes.

LEARN EARLY TO GIVE AND TAKE

KEY POINTS TO REMEMBER

1. In a friendship or relationship, there are some things you should not compromise on. These are the immutable laws; they are too fundamental for you to compromise on.

2. But, for other things, you have to learn to be flexible, to give and take sometimes; but the giving and taking should be on both sides.

3. If you learn to do this early in the friendship, it will ensure peace and understanding, first in your relationship and, subsequently, in your marriage. This will give you peace in your home.

4. If you do not learn to give and take, one of you would have to be subservient all the time, or there would always be disputes.

QUESTIONS TO PONDER

i. Do you agree that, in a relationship or marriage, there should be give and take?

ii. Do you subscribe to the view that the man is the head of the family and, so, whatever decision he makes is final? Does this apply to a relationship even before marriage?

iii. List some of the things (not the immutable laws) which are so dear to your heart that you think you cannot compromise on them at all.

iv. What is the difference between surrender, capitulation and compromise? What is the relevance of each to a relationship or marriage?

CHAPTER 11

Learn the Balancing Act

Sometimes, I wonder whether men and women suit each other. Perhaps they should live next door and visit now and again.

Katherine Hepburn

A male friend of mine complains that, whenever he is going out with his wife, she likes to take her time to dress up. She does not seem to care that she is keeping him waiting while she attends to every minutiae of her dressing, making sure that everything coordinates nicely. When he thinks she has finally finished and is ready to go, that is when she would ask him to come back to the room to help her tie something on her hair or her back. And, when they finally get into the car, she would continue with the dressing up, using the mirror in the car. I tell him that the man next door also complains about the same thing. And so does the neighbour down the road.

A lady complains to me that, whenever her husband comes back from work, he does not want to talk to her. He just sits in front of the TV with the remote in hand and watches the news or sports. Or, he just reads the newspapers, totally ignoring her. I tell her that the lady next door also complains about the same thing. And so does the woman down the road.

Learn the Balancing Act

The foregoing may seem like basic examples, but they reveal fundamental differences between men and women; and any person desiring to have a partner should first learn about these differences. People who are not aware that men and women are wired differently will always find fault with their partners.

They may not realize that what they are complaining about is actually common to just about all men or all women, as the case may be. The secret is to realize this at an early stage and make a serious effort to understand the fundamental differences between men and women. Do this before starting a friendship with the opposite sex, especially if you have marriage in mind.

Fortunately, there are a lot of resources to help you. Perhaps the best selling book on this subject is John Gray's *Men Are from Mars, Women Are from Venus*, first published in 1992. This book has sold more than fifty million copies.

There are many other resources available too. Look for something that suits you, and make it a point to study the fundamental differences between men and women before you venture into any relationship. This will also help you when you start a family. Knowing how boys and girls are wired differently will help you understand why boys are inseparable from their toys or why girls like other pursuits.

Here, we are only referring to a few key differences. Of course, to every rule, there is bound to be an exception; and so it is possible to find a rare breed that is different from the rest of their sex.

Having said that, the following observations would apply to the vast majority of people most of the time:

- ✓ Men love to have their *abilities* recognized and appreciated, whilst women love to have their *feelings* recognized and appreciated.

- ✓ Men prefer to work on their own and exercise their abilities by solving problems quickly and single-handedly. Women, on the other hand, prefer to co-operate and exercise their feelings through interactive communication with one another.

- ✓ When men communicate, they like to go straight to the point. Women, however, are more interested in the conversation, and they hope the point will come out as they talk; there is a bit of speaking in parables.

- ✓ When faced with a tough problem, men withdraw into themselves so that they can focus on how best to solve it. They do not want to tell others about the problem, but women like to talk about it so that others can help them work out a solution.

- ✓ Men prefer to be left alone to sort things out. They do not appreciate sympathy or unsolicited assistance. On the other hand, ladies appreciate sympathy and unsolicited assistance.

- ✓ When a man is under pressure or has just come back tired from work, he is best left alone. He would like to withdraw into himself for a while. This does not mean that he is ignoring his partner or loved one; he just needs space to recharge his batteries.

- ✓ When a woman has something to say, she needs to be listened to. She just needs the attention, not necessarily to be given a solution for her problem.
- ✓ The emotional needs of men and women are very different. When a man is not preoccupied with work, sports or something that engages him, his mind will shift to intimacy, with sex dominating his thoughts.
- ✓ A lady has to be made ready for sex, whereas a man can spring into action easily. She needs to be loved every day and every hour, and be complimented for her looks, appearance, and so on. She needs to hear nice and kind words all the time, especially from the people close to her, such as her partner. Any unkind word—especially from her partner—can seriously affect her self-esteem. Self-esteem is a big thing for ladies, just as much as ego is for men.
- ✓ It is not good enough for a lady to have her partner love her and provide for her; she must hear "I love you" from his lips as often as possible. Some men struggle with this, thinking it is enough that they love their partners and provide for them, and so it is not necessary to put it into words.

Conclusion

I have titled this chapter, "Learn the Balancing Act", because essentially that is what it is—learning to strike a balance between the desires and expectations of men and women. It is actually an issue of wiring, how God wired the sexes even before they were born.

We start life not realizing that the One who created men and women wired them differently. This is not confined to any particular country. It is the same all over, the same in every country and culture, the same in developed and developing countries. This is why, even at an early age, boys behave in certain ways and girls behave in other ways. It is all because of the way the Creator wired us.

The important point is that, once you know yourself very well (as discussed in an earlier chapter) and you know the differences between men and women, you will be better placed to communicate with the opposite sex and deal with issues as they arise.

If a person does not realize that there are fundamental differences between men and women, small issues can easily loom large. I have heard of couples listing a plethora of seemingly minor issues that proved to be big challenges for them.

Some of those marital problems can be traced to their not having an understanding of the fundamental differences between men and women. Hence, they did not make the necessary adjustments to their mindsets. Consequently, they could not see the problem when it was beginning to form.

They could not tell that it was just a matter of one partner understanding the other and making some small adjustments to their mindsets. All that was called for was some balancing act, but they simply did not know that.

They could have nipped many of those issues in the bud, had they known the source of those problems. The Bible says that people perish for lack of knowledge, and the fundamental differences between men and women is one such area[4] where this is happening.

KEY POINTS TO REMEMBER

1. Essentially, men and women are wired differently. They have different "world views". This should be understood and appreciated early by persons preparing to enter into a relationship.
2. The emotional needs of men and women are also different.
3. Men communicate differently from women.
4. Men's expectations are different from women's.

QUESTIONS TO PONDER

i. Pick an aspect of life, such as dressing, and make a list of some differences in approach between yourself and a member or members of the opposite sex.

ii. Have you noticed any fundamental differences between the way your parents handle issues?

iii. Do you have a sibling of the opposite sex? If so, list five fundamental differences between the two of you, in the way you handle issues in the home.

---

[4] *cf. Hosea 4:6*

iv. Make a list of five areas where you have personally experienced men and women looking at issues differently.

v. Do you have a boyfriend or girlfriend? List five fundamental differences between the two of you, in your perspectives and expectations.

vi. List four things about your boyfriend or girlfriend that you are struggling to understand. After reading this chapter, would you consider them to be peculiar to him or her, or could they be characteristic of men or women in general?

CHAPTER 12

Seek Crucial Clearances

God grant me the serenity to accept the things I cannot change, courage to change the things I can, and wisdom to know the difference.

Reinhold Niebuhr, "The Serenity Prayer"

So far so good; the relationship is progressing well, and you are now almost certain that the two of you will make it to the altar. But, remember, you are still at the **Getting to Know You Well stage**. At this point, you may get engaged, if you choose. It is entirely up to you; there are no hard and fast rules about it. However, there are two clearances which both of you must obtain—medical and spiritual. These are crucial in the context of today's world.

Medical clearance

Both of you should go for check-ups for STIs (Sexually Transmitted Infections). From the outside, a person may look healthy, but you do not know what he or she may be carrying inside. In this day and age of HIV/AIDs and other illnesses, I strongly advise that both of you go for check-ups. You should do this together; not each of you going to a separate hospital and then sharing the results with one another. Rather, you should go to the hospital together at the same time, so that you would not have any doubts about each other's results. Moreover, should the need arise, explanations or clarifications can be given by the doctors to the two of you at the same time. This will give you peace of mind.

This is the minimum medical clearance I recommend. If, however, you want to satisfy yourself on other medical issues—for example, whether the man or woman is "normal" in all relevant respects—it is entirely up to you.

Spiritual Clearance

Some people may be asking, what is this? Just as medical clearance is necessary to clear up any medical issues that may be hidden, spiritual clearance is also needed to clear up any spiritual issues that might be hidden in either or both partners.

The aim of this is to ensure that, if there are any demonic forces afflicting either or both partners, they would be exposed and dealt with before the couple are married. This is because, if not dealt with prior to the wedding, those demonic forces would be fighting against the couple at every turn until the marriage collapses.

Some people are free of demonic forces, but others are not. This is not something one can tell from the outside, so it is crucial to have it checked out. If both of you have solid spiritual foundations, as discussed earlier, you would both understand this.

Medical clearance can be obtained from most hospitals. However, spiritual clearance should be obtained only from pastors or prophets with special anointing and deliverance ministries.

Seek Crucial Clearances

We are talking here of ministers who have credibility and a good track record in exposing demons operating inside people and also delivering them. In every country, there are hundreds of pastors and prophets, but only a few of them have the kind of anointing we are talking about here.

Before we go any further, let us look at some situations where we may need spiritual clearances. Contrary to what some people believe, demon possession is real and quite prevalent. It is not confined to any particular segment of society but cuts across all sectors, affecting Christians and non-Christians alike.

Because demonic captivity is not visible, often the people affected may not be aware of it or understand it, or they may be looking in the wrong direction for solutions. When things are not going well, people may come to the conclusion that "there is something wrong in my life," or "something is wrong with me," or words to that effect. But they would have no clue what that "something" might be. Since it is not a medical problem, there would be no physical symptoms to diagnose.

The usual medical way of telling whether there is a physiological, psychological or psychiatric problem is by conducting clinical tests; but that would not be helpful in this case. Sometimes, people in such situations may simply say in their frustration that "luck is not on my side". But luck may have nothing to do with it.

If you are a spiritual person—and especially if you are a member of a church that conducts deliverances or you have seen it done on some Christian TV stations—

you would have at least some awareness of demonic captivity or oppression. You would also probably know that demonic oppression does not happen only to non-believers. On the contrary, Christians—and born-again Christians for that matter—have been victims of demonic oppression too.

Mary Magdalene, for example, was under demonic captivity; the Bible tells us that Jesus cast seven demons cast out of her.[5] Even more severely possessed was the man living in the Gerasenes region, whom Jesus delivered from a legion of demons. Prior to his deliverance, he had become so abnormal that he could no longer live in society but had been driven to living in the tombs; in fact, he had not worn clothes for a very long time. He used to cut himself with stones and had become so violent that he could break the chains put on him.[6]

Not only adults, but even children can be oppressed by demons. A Greek woman sought Jesus' help for her daughter, who was severely demon-possessed[7], and Jesus delivered the girl out of demonic captivity.

A boy, the only child of his parents, was so severely oppressed that Jesus' disciples could not heal him. An evil spirit used to make him go into convulsions, knocking him down and throwing him about. The evil spirit would often knock him into the fire or water, with intent to destroy him. The boy's father told Jesus that his son had

---

[5] *cf. Luke 8:2*
[6] *cf. Mark 5:1-20; Luke 8:26-39*
[7] *cf. Mark 7:24-30; Matthew 15:21-28*

been possessed by the demon since childhood.[8] Jesus terminated that captivity by commanding the deaf and dumb spirit to leave the child.

Such demonic activities are also taking place today. Even some pastors and prophets have been known to be demon-possessed or victims of demonic attacks. Some Christians struggle to come to terms with the possibility that they could be victims of demonic oppression. But deliverance experiences in various countries have shown beyond a doubt that even a born-again Christian could be afflicted by demonic forces, and this may not be known until the person has an encounter with a pastor or prophet gifted in deliverances. Particularly in the context of relationships and marriage, dreams can be helpful in revealing demonic oppression:

- ✓ If someone comes to make love to you in your dreams, and you are not even married, it can mean that you are either possessed or seriously afflicted by evil spirits or demonic forces. You have what is called a "spiritual husband" or "spiritual wife" (sometimes also referred to as a "night husband" or "night wife"). This spiritual spouse comes to make love to you because you are "married" to it in the spirit realm.

    You may not know how this came about or even understand it, but the reality is that this spirit being that comes to make love to you is doing so because it is "married" to you in the spirit world; there is a "legal marriage" between the two of you.

---

[8] *cf. Mark 9:17-29*

In some cases, you will see the same face all the time and, as soon as it shows up in your sleep, you know who it is. In other cases, the spiritual spouse will keep changing faces, and so it may appear to you as if different beings are coming to make love to you. But, in actual fact, it is the same spirit being, only that it is capable of disguising itself to deceive you.

✓ Sometimes, in your dreams, you may see yourself wearing a wedding ring on your ring finger—when, in real life, you do not wear a ring at all, because you are not even engaged, let alone married. In some cases, you may see yourself wearing other attractive jewelry as well.

It is important to understand that, whether you like it or not, you have a relationship with a spirit being; and it is based on this relationship that this being comes to make love to you in your dreams. Make no mistake about it, you are a captive of that spirit being, and it controls your life and destiny. Because you are under demonic captivity, in your dreams you seem to be a willing participant in the love-making—and you probably enjoy every bit of it!

It is after you wake up from your sleep and realize what has happened that you become upset in your physical self. But you are powerless on your own to put an end to it. The dreams are just pointers to what is happening in your spiritual life; the spirit being would be very busy undermining or interfering in your life generally, especially your attempts to find a suitable life-partner in the natural world.

One of the consequences of this is that this spiritual (or night) spouse will prevent you from getting married in the natural because, as far as it is concerned, you are "legally married" to it (in the spirit realm). Hence, it would jealously protect its "marriage" and deal harshly with any interference by anybody, including yourself. It would not tolerate your attempts to have a relationship with a life partner in the natural, because the spirit being would interpret it to mean that you are "cheating" on your marriage or trying to "divorce" it in favour of that other person.

Of course, many people in such situations may not even be aware that they are in demonic captivity or realize what is happening to them. So they will not, for example, understand why they can never get married; why every time they meet somebody interested in having a relationship with them in the natural, things do not seem to work out; why that person, who was initially so interested, suddenly cuts them off completely, and the relationship becomes a non-starter; or, if it does take off, before long it fizzles out.

All of a sudden, phone calls are no longer answered and email communication halts. This is because the spirit being is operating against the budding friendship and doing all it can to stop it, such as creating confusion, mistrust or other problems between the partners—and before long it is all over. The spirit being would be very happy about this, as it would mean that it remains in control and is the only spouse to the person in demonic captivity.

People in captivity to their spiritual spouses may be going through this scenario over and over again, without the faintest idea about what is happening to them. But, at least, they would know that somebody comes to make love to them in their dreams and they are powerless to resist or stop that being.

- ✓ Even if you succeeded in getting married in the natural, the spiritual (or night) spouse would torment you and your marriage relationship so relentlessly that the marriage would fail. This is because the spiritual spouse considers your "marriage" to it (in the spirit) to be legally binding.

Some people in such situations get so tormented that they go from one failed relationship or marriage to the next, and yet they have no idea what is happening to them. All they can point to are minor issues in the relationship that inexplicably became such huge problems that they caused the couple to break up. In some cases, quarrels and fights become the order of the day, with no end in sight.

Some people do not experience any bliss for even a decent period in the relationship or marriage, all because the spiritual spouse is actively working against the marriage. They do not realize that all their problems have been orchestrated in the spirit by the jealous spiritual spouse. Once the damage is done in the spirit, it merely manifests in the physical realm. (Bear in mind what we said earlier, that things happen first in the spirit realm, and that the spirit realm controls the natural realm.)

SEEK CRUCIAL CLEARANCES

The worst case scenario is where both partners have spiritual spouses. In such cases, the relationship (or marriage) hangs on tenterhooks, and peace and tranquility become only brief passing phases. Let the truth be told: there are such marriages, where the husband and wife wonder how they could have got it so wrong. But the fact is that they did not get it wrong; what is wrong is the spiritual spouse coming between them and undermining their marriage.

Some of these marriages last for only a short time; others longer, but with the couples in pain, stress and depression. In some cases, the marriage has become an empty shell, with the spouses living independent lives. To all outward appearances, they are a married couple; but, in private, they are living in separate rooms at home.

Through it all, the husband and wife may be totally ignorant that their marriage is under demonic attack. They have no idea whatsoever that all their troubles and fights are actually being orchestrated by spirit beings opposing their marriage. This is really the root cause of their problems. Given the right help (such as through confidential counselling), they are likely to be able to save their marriage when the truth is revealed to them.

✓ The spiritual spouse might also try to break up the human couple's marriage by making sure they remain childless. The spirit being could render either partner or both of them barren, as it knows that this would weaken the marriage and lead to its collapse—

thereby leaving the spirit being to have its spiritual spouse all to itself. In the case of a man, the spirit being might make him impotent so that he cannot sustain an erection, let alone satisfy his wife or father a child. This would obviously have disastrous consequences for the marriage.

Thus, any time the man (or his wife) wants to make love, the spirit being would render the husband impotent, so that the love-making becomes an occasion for disappointment and sadness. But immediately the human husband goes to sleep, the spiritual (or night) husband would come to give the woman a really good one in her dreams. This would undoubtedly have the effect of drawing the wife closer to the one in her dreams and farther away from her human husband.

This can also happen to the man, with his spiritual (night) wife calling the shots, thereby putting an enormous strain on the marriage.

✓ The spiritual (night) wife might also try to wreck the human couple's marriage by causing the husband to have a low or zero sperm count, so that the human wife is unable to get pregnant. The husband and wife would be going from one doctor to another, doing all that the doctors recommend, but there would be no improvement in the man's sperm count. In this case, even though the husband and wife may enjoy love-making, the spiritual spouse would have frustrated their plans to have a child.

- ✓ The spirit being could also try to take away the couple's affection for each other. This might affect only one partner in the marriage or in some cases both. The attraction which the partners had for each other in the beginning would gradually disappear. They would come to the point where one or both of them would not have any love left for the other, and they would not understand why this has happened. Worse, they could be turned off the other partner or even feel an intense dislike or hatred for him or her.

  One or both of them could lose interest in the marriage and start looking elsewhere for love. They would not have the foggiest idea that all this is the result of the spiritual spouse gradually working on one or both of them until all the affection is gone from the marriage. Without affection, all talk of making love becomes out of the question.

  The marriage would be suffering, going downhill, but the spiritual spouse would be jubilant, as it would have succeeded in drawing its "spouse" closer and closer to it. In the natural, the marriage partners would not be able to explain what is happening to them. They would be pointing accusing fingers at one another, when in fact they are the innocent parties.

  Sometimes, in the case of an unmarried person, the spiritual spouse could cause the person to lose all interest in forming a relationship with the opposite sex. Such a person may look perfectly normal on the outside and may even be an eligible bachelor or lady, as the case may be. But, inside, he or she is being controlled by a spiritual spouse. In fact, such people may have an attractive façade, but, within, they are devoid of affection. If it is a lady, she would get turned off by men; and, if it is a man, he would be turned off by ladies. Of course, not everyone who shuns human relationships is in the grip of demonic captivity; there may be other explanations for the person's behaviour.

One sure way of finding out if someone is being controlled by a spiritual spouse is by asking about his or her dreams. The curious thing—which most of these people would not be saying to others because of the shame and embarrassment involved—is that, though they have no affection at all for the opposite sex in the natural, they make love regularly in their dreams and enjoy doing so. They have no control over this and do not actually understand what is happening to them. It is all because they are in demonic captivity.

✓ A further indication of demonic captivity is when a lady regularly dreams that she has a home with children. In her dreams, she has beautiful children she loves to play with. But, in the natural, she may not have any children at all (in many cases) or she may have more children in her dreams than in real life. This means that the lady has a spiritual husband, and it is he who is preventing the lady from having any or more children in the natural.

The children the lady plays with in her dreams are those she has with the spiritual (or night) husband; and those spirit children would be staying in their "home" in the spirit world, which could be a river, sea or forest—the usual abode of such spirit beings.

Summary on spiritual clearance

A person may appear perfectly normal but may, in fact, be demon-possessed or afflicted by demonic forces. If this is not discovered before marriage and deliverance effected, there could be lots of trouble on the way.

First, those demonic forces may prevent the relationship from maturing into a marriage. The partners may find themselves embroiled in quarrels, arguments and other problems, and they might not understand why.

Secondly, the marriage may take place, but it might move from one problem to another, with the parties having no clue as to the real cause. Eventually, the marriage could collapse, and the partners would not be able to understand what went wrong.

It is better to avoid this altogether by going for spiritual clearance. If it is discovered that demonic forces are operating against one or both partners, deliverance would have to take place to set the party or parties free.

What if the results are negative?

If the medical tests show that a partner has one or more diseases that are curable, then it goes without saying that he or she has to seek treatment to be healed. The same applies to other medical deficiencies which may be discovered in one or both partners. If, on the other hand, a partner is found to be infected with more serious diseases (such as HIV or AIDs) that could have serious implications for the marriage, the other partner may consider withdrawing altogether from the relationship.

Alternatively, the parties may decide to go for healing and deliverance. In such a case, they may set a deadline by which, if the infected partner does not find healing or deliverance, the party not carrying the disease may choose to withdraw from the relationship.

Similarly, if spiritual clearance cannot be obtained because a partner is demon-possessed or afflicted by demonic forces, the parties should ask for deliverance so that the person can be set free. After that, the way would be clear for them to get married. If there is no deliverance, demonic forces would be working actively against the marriage to destroy it, as we have discussed in this chapter. However, if the person who is demon-possessed does not wish to go for deliverance (for example, does not believe in it), the other party will have grounds to withdraw from the relationship.

KEY POINTS TO REMEMBER

1. Before getting to the altar, the parties should make sure that there are no medical or spiritual barriers which could undermine the marriage.

2. If tests show that a partner has curable medical diseases or deficiencies, these should be addressed without delay.

3. If, however, the tests show that a partner has an incurable disease, the other partner may consider withdrawing from the relationship altogether, or the parties may go for healing and deliverance.

4. On the spiritual side, if a partner is demon-possessed, deliverance has to be effected to set the person free before proceeding with the marriage.

5. If, however, the demon-possessed person does not go for deliverance, the other party may withdraw from the relationship and not proceed with the marriage.

QUESTIONS TO PONDER

i. Do you agree that medical and spiritual clearances are crucial before deciding whether to get married or not?

ii. How would you respond if the person you have fallen in love with—and want to marry—is found to have a severe disease that may seriously affect the marriage?

iii. Do you believe a Christian can be demon-possessed?

iv. Do you believe in healing and deliverance?

v. Do you know of a pastor or prophet who has a good track record in conducting healing and deliverance?

vi. If the person you intended to marry is not healed or delivered (after a few attempts), would you still love him or her? Would you still proceed with the marriage?

PART E

PREPARING FOR MARRIAGE

CHAPTER 13

Start Marriage Preparations

The secret to having a good marriage is to understand that marriage must be total, it must be permanent, and it must be equal.
    Frank Pittman

Once you have obtained the necessary medical and spiritual clearances, the way is clear for the two of you to get married. If you are not already engaged, this is a good time to do so.

You should start making plans for the marriage now: the type of wedding you want, where it is going to be held, and where you are going for your honeymoon. Carefully study the various options and what you can afford before making a choice. Make sure that you keep within your budget and do not borrow heavily to finance a lavish wedding. There are numerous stories of couples who spent beyond their means, just so they could have "the wedding of the year". They put on very big shows, only to find out—a bare few weeks later—that they could not pay their bills... and then everything started to fall apart.

Next, you should plan your spiritual life. If you are already worshipping together at the same church and you intend to go on doing so, then half the problem is solved.

If, however, you are not already worshipping at the same church, then you have to make a decision on this—where you will be worshipping together. You will also have to discuss how you can attend fellowship meetings and bible classes together, which church ministries you will each be serving in, and so on.

Most importantly, your marriage preparations should include discussions on how you can help each other grow spiritually and establish a home in which Jesus Christ is indeed the head. Don't forget that, up to this point, you have never lived together, and so you do not have any experience in this area. So you have to discuss how you can come together to pray, fast, do devotions, and so on.

You should also make plans about where you will live. Are you going to rent first and buy a house later? If so, you should start planning for this. Or, do you already have a property you can move into? It is the responsibility of the man to provide accommodation for the couple, and so he should be taking the lead in making the plans and sharing them with his partner.

I have heard of some men who got married and took their wives to live in the same house with their parents because they have a large house with many rooms in it. I do not recommend this. As newly-weds, the couple should have all their independence, freedom and privacy for the marriage to develop on its own. You do not need interference from parents (or other relations).

Start Marriage Preparations

Moving into your parents' house with your wife (or husband) is fraught with risks. Thus, although the lure of free accommodation and other freebies may be strong, it must be strongly resisted. The newly married husband and wife should start life on their own and shoulder their own responsibilities. If a couple cannot afford to have a place of their own, it means that they are not ready for marriage, and so they should wait until they are financially independent.

Another thing which you have to come to terms with is how to manage your finances. If only one person is working, how is that one salary going to be managed? If, on the other hand, both partners are income-earners (as it is in many cases today), the question again will be, how are you going to manage your finances? Budgeting, financial management, and related questions pose challenges to many couples in today's world. As a matter of fact, it is believed that many marriages have failed mainly because of disputes over money. Some churches offer seminars and counselling on these matters. Please take full advantage of them and learn the basics.

Opinions differ as to whether the couple should have only one joint account or whether each of them can have their own individual account in addition to a joint account. In the latter case, they will have to decide what should go into the joint account and what can be retained in the individual accounts. You will need to discuss this matter fully with your partner and come to an agreement prior to the marriage.

I have heard of situations where, immediately upon marriage, the couple went and bought themselves a very nice apartment, a brand new car, and brand new furniture. Everything in the house was brand new, because they wanted to start life all anew.

This was impressive, but the only problem was that it was all bought on credit—a mortgage for the apartment, another mortgage for the car, and store and credit cards for the other purchases. Thus, they got themselves entangled in debt—huge debt.

Thereafter, all their focus was on how to service those debts. Romance took a backseat, and all the other things they had enjoyed doing before stopped happening, because they could not afford them anymore. I do not think I need to say any more; you can imagine what became of their marriage.

Key Points to Remember

1. Once you have obtained your medical and spiritual clearances, you can start making preparations for the marriage. You may get engaged, if you have not already done so.

2. You should not leave marriage preparations until the last minute, as it could be a logistics nightmare. You should start your preparations well ahead of the wedding date.

3. You should take advantage of pre-marital counselling programmes and seminars offered by your church.
4. You will also need education and counselling on the basics of budgeting, financial planning, and money management.
5. You have to make decisions as to where you will live together as a couple—whether to rent or buy your own place—and where you will worship together.

QUESTIONS TO PONDER

i. What kind of wedding would you like?

ii. Should you and your partner have only one joint account into which all your earnings would go? Or should you have individual accounts? Why?

iii. Upon marriage, would you like to rent for a while or buy your own place straightaway?

iv. Would you consider buying a house together? Why or why not?

v. Would you accept an offer by one of your parents to fund the whole wedding? Why or why not?

CHAPTER 14

Follow Family Protocol

"Honour your father and mother"—which is the first commandment with a promise—"so that it may go well with you and that you may enjoy long life on the earth."

Ephesians 6:2-3, NIV

Get your families' blessings for the marriage

You will recall that, when you were about to enter the **Getting to Know You Well stage**, you had to inform your parents (or someone with authority over you) about your newly-formed relationship; and your partner had to do the same too. No doubt, from time to time, they would have been asking you how things were going between the two of you. Now that you have made up your mind to get married, you should formally inform them of your decision and get their blessings.

As God's people who are walking the walk with Him, you are not to take your respective parents for granted. Ask for their blessings, and expect them to actually pray with and for you and grant you their blessings. In other words, they should not merely give you the go-ahead to marry but pray for you and wish you every success in the proposed marriage.

Follow family protocol

Every family has its own protocol which must be followed when it comes to marriage matters. This is especially so with the lady, as she is the one whose "hand" has to be "asked for" in marriage. She is also the one who has to be "given away". Hence, it is important to follow her family's protocol. It is her family who have brought her up to be what she is today, and so they have to be respected and honoured. If you want the girl, then you have to follow their protocol. By now, you should know all of their requirements and expectations, anyway.

You may not like some of their requirements, but consider this: first, you have already been made fully aware of them (or should have been); and, secondly, you have decided to marry her with that full knowledge. That said, you are still free to pull out of the relationship if you no longer wish to go ahead (provided it is not based on some flimsy excuse).

If they want a traditional wedding...

In some countries or cultures, the lady's family may insist on having a traditional wedding in addition to the church wedding. Typically, this would involve some kind of ceremony, followed by a feast in which many guests are invited and the lady is formally "given away". As far as the family is concerned, once all these formalities are completed, she has been married off to the man.

If a couple bypass these cultural dictates and rush off to have a Christian wedding in church, some families would consider it an affront to their community and culture, and they may withhold their blessings. To such families, until the traditional wedding is held publicly and celebrated, the couple is not considered properly married. A couple who find themselves in such a situation would have lots of problems with their families, especially their extended families.

KEY POINTS TO REMEMBER

1. It is important to have the blessings of both families before the partners proceed to hold their wedding.

2. It is also important to follow family protocol. It is the protocol of the lady's family which is more important in this case, because she is the one whose "hand" has be "asked for" in marriage. If their protocol is not followed, the families may decide not to give their approval to the partners to go ahead with the wedding.

3. If the man's side also has a protocol to be followed, then the couple will have to comply with the protocols of both sides. But it is the protocol of the lady's side which is more important in this context.

4. If the lady comes from a cultural background that requires a traditional wedding to be held (in addition to the Christian wedding), this has to be followed too.

QUESTIONS TO PONDER

i. Should Christian couples go straight to church for their wedding and not pay any attention to cultural dictates?

ii. Would you consider having a wedding in church first and then holding a traditional wedding ceremony as well?

iii. How would you react if your partner refuses to participate in a traditional marriage or comply with other cultural dictates? Why?

CHAPTER 15

Finish with God's Blessings

Let us come before His presence with thanksgiving; Let us shout joyfully to Him with psalms. For the LORD is the great God, and the great King above all gods.

Psalm 95:2-3

The usual route to marriage for many Christians is to hold a wedding in church. They will go through the ceremony (a white wedding), with a pastor presiding over an audience made up of their family and friends. When they have made their vows to God and each other, the pastor will pronounce them married. Then they become husband and wife, with the blessings of God as well as the church.

These days, however, couples tend to be more innovative and adventurous. Thus, some may decide to have their wedding on a beach or riverbank, or at a park or some other non-traditional setting. What is important is to have a pastor perform the ceremony and the couple's family and friends there to celebrate the marriage.

For one reason or another, other couples may not want a wedding ceremony of any kind at all. They may simply choose to have a civil marriage—going to the city council registry, following its requirements, and obtaining an official marriage certificate.

Finish with God's Blessings

However, for Christians, it is still important to get the blessings of God. Whichever way the couple choose to tie the knot, they need the finishing touch of God's blessings upon their marriage. This may be done by having the marriage blessed by a pastor in a small church ceremony; without this, the marriage cannot be considered to have the blessings of God.

It should be emphasized here that cohabitation cannot be blessed by a church or a pastor. This is because cohabitation (without the commitment of marriage) is contrary to the Word of God—even though the law in some countries may accept cohabitation to be as good as marriage.

In fact, it is considered a sin for a man and woman to live together and do all the things that a husband and wife do, without being formally married. Therefore, if a couple are cohabiting and they want the blessings of God, they will have to abandon their sinful relationship, ask for forgiveness, and get married. They can then seek God's blessings for their life together.

A believer cannot afford to miss out on God's blessings for something as important as marriage, which is meant to last a lifetime. Thus, it is incumbent on all believers to ensure that their marriage gets God's blessings to start with.

Key Points to Remember

1. Every Christian couple needs to obtain God's blessings for their marriage.

2. God's blessings may be obtained by having a pastor bless the marriage before the couple commence life together.

3. Where believers have yet to obtain the blessings of God, their marriage cannot be considered complete—even if the couple have been pronounced husband and wife in some other way. The blessings of God will put a seal on the marriage.

4. Cohabitation—which is permitted by law in some countries—cannot be blessed by a church or a pastor, because it is contrary to the Word of God.

Questions to Ponder

i. Which would you prefer: a church wedding or some other option, such as marrying at a civil registry? Why?

ii. What type of marriage ceremony would you like: a grand wedding or a small family affair?

iii. What type of honeymoon would you like? Would you like your honeymoon to be at home or abroad?

CHAPTER 16

Don't Allow Yourself to Get Desperate

Wait on the LORD; *be of good courage,*
And He shall strengthen your heart;
Wait, I say, on the LORD!

Psalm 27:14

Searching for a life partner is no easy thing. It can be challenging and frustrating at times. If you have a "childhood sweetheart" from your schooldays or someone you grew up with (perhaps in your church or neighbourhood), you will have a huge lead over others. This is especially so if your respective families have been aware of your budding friendship and have no problems with it.

Nevertheless, it is still highly recommended that you follow the guidelines given in this book. In particular, make a checklist of the inner beauty traits you desire in a life partner and filter this person through it to see if he or she really meets your personal standards. Be careful not to draw up the checklist to favour the person you already know—it should be the other way around.

For most people, however, they have to start from scratch in their search for a life partner. It will not be all smooth sailing; the quest to find "the right one" is a journey that can be littered with disappointments, frustrations, and sometimes pain and sadness. If this is happening to you, please do not take it too personally. Do not think there is something wrong with you.

If you are a man, do not think that girls dislike you or deem you as not handsome or eligible. Similarly, if you are a lady, please do not think that you are unattractive to men or that they consider you to be unworthy of them or "not wife material". Generally speaking, it is not like that at all.

What matters is for you to find your match. That person is somewhere out there. It is only a matter of time before you meet each other. The timing and circumstances under which you will meet are in God's hands—which is why it is important to make God your primary focus and do the things which will enable you to achieve your purpose in life and your destiny.

Putting God first is more important than anything else and, once you dedicate yourself to Him and His purpose for you, the burden and pressure of looking for someone to start a relationship with will go away. The right one will turn up when you least expect it. Your life partner is definitely out there somewhere—it is simply a matter of your paths crossing, and then bingo!

Be patient, be persistent

In the course of searching for a partner, sometimes desperation might set in—especially if you are in a hurry, but you cannot seem to find that person who meets your standards quickly, and this has dragged on for some time.

Don't Allow Yourself to Get Desperate

There may be seasons when you cannot seem to find anyone suitable at all and you start to wonder if you are searching in the right places or not.

In some cases, finding someone to start with is not difficult but, after a short while, things get cold—he (or she) does not answer the phone, emails are not replied to, and other moves made by you are repelled. What has started as an extremely promising relationship soon fades away. Sometimes, this happens after the friendship has been going on for a while.

With these kinds of experiences, you go through the proverbial one step forward, three steps back. Just when you thought you were making progress on a friendship that could one day turn into a relationship and marriage, you suddenly find yourself back to square one.

You begin to look at yourself and wonder if something is wrong with you. It is a good idea at this juncture to do a self-evaluation, because there may be one or two things you need to adjust. Maybe you are too aggressive, or the other way round. Or, maybe, you need to change your choice of words. For each and every one of us, there is always room for improvement.

Having said that, I want you to understand that those experiences may not necessarily reflect negatively on you. Consider them as normal or usual; many people go through similar situations in some measure or other before finding the right one for them.

The danger is that, if one is too much in a hurry to find a life partner, one could become desperate. It is often said that desperate people do desperate things. Hence, if you allow yourself to become desperate, you would no longer act rationally; you would shift from following the principles we have been teaching in this book and end up marrying in haste—and repenting at leisure. Surely you have heard the saying, "rush in, rush out"?

If you allow yourself to become desperate, you would be tempted to lower your own standards. My strong advice is that you should not get yourself into such a situation. Focus on your relationship with God and your purpose in this life; this should be your number one priority. In the course of doing so, you will surely meet someone suitable. In fact, your life partner may be just around the corner. There is definitely someone out there for you, someone who meets most of your expectations on inner as well as outer beauty.

You can keep desperation in check by not being overly fixated with searching for a partner. By all means, keep your eyes open in case you run into or cross the path of someone suitable; but don't let that be your focus.

Be positive at all times; use positive language. Use your faith and call things into being as if they were. These are key godly principles which should not depart from you. When they do, that is when desperation will set in.

KEY POINTS TO REMEMBER

1. It is the exception rather than the norm for a person to find a life partner easily and quickly, unless the partner is a childhood or school sweetheart.

2. The quest for a life-partner can take many twists and turns and can be littered with challenges, setbacks and even frustrations. Do not be discouraged or start to blame yourself if your initial attempts to find a partner prove unfruitful.

3. Be persistent, but have your primary focus on God and your purpose in life. As you do so, your life partner will turn up.

4. Finding a life partner requires a lot of patience; it is not a race but a marathon.

5. It is dangerous to allow yourself to become desperate because, once that happens, you might be tempted to do desperate things, and people will take advantage of you or even think you have lost it. You could become bitter as a result.

QUESTIONS TO PONDER

i. Have you started looking for a life partner yet?

ii. How long are you prepared to search?

iii. Have you already got some strategies in mind as to how you will go about it?

iv. Would you be prepared to travel overseas in search of a partner?

v. How would you ensure you do not get frustrated and desperate?

vi. Do you know anyone who has been searching for a very long time but cannot seem to find the right one? Have you had a chance to talk to this person and find out why?

The End...
And the Beginning of a
New Life Together!

About the Author

Dr Nii Lante Wallace-Bruce is an international evangelist, author and lawyer. He holds a PhD in law from the University of Sydney and was in legal practice for many years before moving to the University of Western Australia, where he held a tenured position for more than a decade.

Dr Wallace-Bruce has travelled to many countries. He was with the Max Planck Institute for International and Public Law in Heidelberg, Germany, for some time and until recently worked with the United Nations.

Anointed to preach the Word of God with passion, power and authority, the author has ministered as an international evangelist in a number of countries. He has also written many books, including faith-based Christian books.

Your Next Step

This book is one of a series. In order to get the complete picture on relationships and marriage, you ought to read the whole series.

The next volume is on *Enjoying a Godly Marriage*.

www.ingramcontent.com/pod-product-compliance
Lightning Source LLC
Chambersburg PA
CBHW061657040426
42446CB00010B/1789